The Cycling
ANTHOLOGY

VOLUME THREE

Edited by
Ellis Bacon
&
Lionel Birnie

YELLOW JERSEY PRESS
LONDON

Published by Yellow Jersey Press 2014

2 4 6 8 10 9 7 5 3 1

Copyright © Peloton Publishing 2013

Each author has asserted their right under the Copyright, Designs
and Patents Act 1988 to be identified as the author of their work

First published in Great Britain in 2013 by
Peloton Publishing

Yellow Jersey Press
Random House, 20 Vauxhall Bridge Road,
London SW1V 2SA

www.vintage-books.co.uk

Addresses for companies within The Random House Group Limited can be
found at: www.randomhouse.co.uk/offices.htm

The Random House Group Limited Reg. No. 954009

A CIP catalogue record for this book
is available from the British Library

ISBN 9780224092456

The Random House Group Limited supports the Forest Stewardship
Council® (FSC®), the leading international forest-certification organisation.
Our books carrying the FSC label are printed on FSC®-certified paper.
FSC is the only forest-certification scheme supported by the
leading environmental organisations, including Greenpeace.
Our paper procurement policy can be found at:
www.randomhouse.co.uk/environment

Printed and bound by Clays Ltd, St Ives plc

THE CYCLING ANTHOLOGY

THE CYCLING ANTHOLOGY

THE NEUTRALISED ZONE

INTRODUCTION BY THE EDITORS

Welcome to the third volume of *The Cycling Anthology*, which marks a successful first year for our co-operative project, showcasing the work of some of the best cycling writers.

Following our Tour de France special edition, this volume looks back at the 2013 season.

Inevitably, the fall-out from Lance Armstrong's admission to Oprah Winfrey that he had doped throughout his seven-year reign at the Tour de France cast a deep shadow over professional cycling in 2013.

While the sport wrestled with the consequences of Armstrong's confession, there was nevertheless much to enjoy.

Our thanks to all of our contributors for their continued support for *The Cycling Anthology*. Our very special thanks go to all our readers. We hope you enjoy this latest collection of original writing.

Ellis Bacon & Lionel Birnie

1

David Zabriskie, Tom Danielson and Christian Vande Velde finally admitted to the public that they had doped in the wake of the USADA investigation.

All three had privately confessed years earlier, had been repentant and were following a clean road, yet they faced a rocky reception when they returned to racing.

Neal Rogers asks whether they deserved to be treated more leniently than riders who are caught red-handed, serve their ban and return as if nothing had happened.

THE CURIOUS CASE OF
THE GARMIN THREE

BY NEAL ROGERS

When the United States Anti-Doping Agency released its reasoned decision on October 10th, 2012 – a 1,000-page dossier of evidence proving widespread, systematic doping by Lance Armstrong, Johan Bruyneel, Michele Ferrari and a dozen former US Postal Service team riders – reaction ran across the spectrum of emotion.

Armstrong loyalists, awed by his unprecedented seven consecutive Tour de France victories, enthralled by his role in the cancer community, or starstruck by his celebrity status, were angry, and crestfallen.

American cycling fans, who had long revered former US national champions such as George Hincapie and Levi Leipheimer, expressed shock, disappointment, and sadness.

The doping problem, which American fans had long viewed as a cultural issue within the European peloton, could no longer be viewed as an overseas phenomenon.

If the past indiscretions of Tyler Hamilton and Floyd Landis had not been enough, there was no

denying the depth of deceit that had been part of
American cycling, extending over a decade. The best
Americans of their generations weren't just cheaters, they were the best cheaters in a peloton that had
been, for over 20 years, devoid of a moral compass.
The Americans had gone to Europe, discovered doping, and perfected the art; Armstrong had benefitted
more than anyone.

And while Armstrong, Hamilton, Landis, Hincapie and Leipheimer would never again compete
after the USADA report was released, that wasn't the
case for 'The Garmin Three': a trio of active riders
– Christian Vande Velde, David Zabriskie and Tom
Danielson – who seemingly fell into a category of
their own.

Between them were Grand Tour stage wins, week-
long stage race titles and national championships. As
the USADA report proved, and their scripted, simul-
taneously-released confessional apologies confirmed,
all three riders had cheated for years, and reaped the
benefits. This was not in question.

But all three had done something the majority
of their peers had not; they'd changed their ways,
willingly, well before being exposed, well before a
federal investigation had been launched, well before
the pro peloton began to collectively recognise that
it had been poisoning itself – its viability, its future
– from within, one injection, one blood transfusion
at a time.

Beginning in the summer of 2007, under the leadership of team manager Jonathan Vaughters – also a former US Postal rider, and who also admitted to doping – Vande Velde, Zabriskie and Danielson agreed to leave behind both their respective teams and their sinful pasts.

For the 2008 season and beyond, they accepted the option that they would likely face defeat, on the playing field, for victory of another sense: the kind that enables one to sleep easier at night, knowing that they'd done the right thing – if not initially, then while they still had the chance to do it on their own terms.

* * *

On stage four of the 2013 Giro d'Italia, the race was spared a potentially awkward moment when 23-year-old Enrico Battaglin, of the UCI Pro Continental team Bardiani Valvole-CSF Inox, took victory in Serra San Bruno.

Just moments earlier, it appeared as though Italian Danilo Di Luca, of Vini Fantini-Selle Italia, might take the stage win. The rider known as 'The Killer' had launched an audacious attack on the second and final rated climb, and drove to the finish line with young Colombian rider Robinson Chalapud. The pair pushed over the summit with nearly 20 seconds on the main group, but were caught with 600 metres to go. In the chaos that followed, across wet and slippery stone slabs, Battaglin timed his sprint to perfection to upset the sport's biggest names, including the race leader, Katusha's Luca Paolini.

An underdog had won, and, perhaps equally importantly, Di Luca had not.

Di Luca, 37, won the Giro in 2007, and finished second overall in 2009. He also served suspensions during both of those seasons – in 2007, for prior involvement with Italian doping doctor Carlo Santuccione, and in 2009, when he tested positive for using the blood-booster CERA during that year's Giro. He also delivered a urine sample during his 2007 Giro victory that reportedly recorded the hormone levels of a small child, dubbed *pipi degli angeli* (angel's pee) – a sign of the use of masking agents. He was ultimately cleared for that offence, with Italian Olympic Committee anti-doping officials admitting there was 'not a sufficient degree of probability' for a doping conviction. Each time, like so many others, he denied any wrongdoing. He was able to keep his 2007 Giro title, though he was stripped of his 2009 second place.

After serving a suspension, Di Luca returned in 2011 with Katusha, riding for no salary. Then he rode a season with Acqua & Sapone, and opened his 2013 campaign after signing with Vini Fantini in late April, just before the Giro began.

By comparison, Battaglin was an unheralded young rider, a distant nephew of Giovanni Battaglin, the 1981 Giro and Vuelta champion. He won the prestigious Coppa Sabatini in 2011, as a *stagiaire*, or apprentice rider, beating another disgraced doper, Davide Rebellin, who was returning after being stripped of his 2008 Olympic silver medal for using CERA.

That evening, in Serra San Bruno, I wrote a commentary piece titled 'Why Battaglin's Giro stage win matters'.

'Just as it's naïve to think that doping in cycling is a thing of the past, it's also unrealistic to wish that the riders who contributed to the damage the sport now faces would just fade away,' I wrote. 'Whether or not these riders, or Di Luca, are now respecting the doping regulations they disregarded in the past is impossible to know. Performances, by and large, are more believable than they were even five years ago. Times are slower, attacks are less dramatic, and time gaps are closer. While his move was bold, that Di Luca was unable to hold his attack is encouraging.

'The day when the pro peloton is clear of suspicion will likely never materialise,' I concluded. 'However, the day when the peloton is clear of riders with controversial pasts may be only a few years away. Until then, it's understandable that many will prefer to cheer for the underdog – the rider with a clean record and the possibility of a clean slate. Sometimes, he may even win.'

Reaction, on Twitter and in the *VeloNews.com* comments section, was mixed. Some applauded the stance I'd taken. Others did not, and accused me of nationalism, of holding American riders who had doped to one standard, and Europeans, such as Di Luca, to another.

'This strikes me as hypocritical and simple-minded stuff from Neal Rogers, cheering Di Luca's getting caught by young unknown riders who have yet to be caught in any doping dragnets,' one commenter said. 'Garmin is packed full of "riders with controversial pasts". Let's see if he has the same venom for them as they defend their Giro title.'

The last sentence was a reference to Ryder Hesjedal's victory at the 2012 Giro – the biggest-ever win for the Garmin-Sharp team.

A few nights later, a British colleague brought up my article, and essentially posed the same question to me. I'll paraphrase: 'Di Luca doped. Rebellin doped. Valverde doped. So did Vande Velde, Zabriskie, and Danielson. What's the difference? Why do some riders receive different treatment for essentially committing the same crime as others?'

The critical difference, I said, was not the crime, but what they had done in the time that followed. The critical difference was that Garmin's riders had ac-knowledged, and apologised for, their transgressions. The critical difference, I said, would not be found where the rules had been broken, but through the course of actions that had been taken in the months and years since the line had been crossed.

* * *

That 'The Garmin Three' had doped before joining the team was the worst-kept secret in the pro cycling universe. The team seemed to be an amnesty organisation for rehabilitated cheaters, a safe haven for riders who had been caught up in the Wild West doping heyday of the late 1990s and early 2000s, and had decided enough was enough.

The Garmin team was an agent for change in the long term – in the short term it was a means of redemption for riders who hoped to reverse what seemed to be irreversible. They could not go back in time and change their misdeeds, so the Garmin riders did the next best thing, by creating an atmosphere where younger riders would not face the same difficult choices.

'We found each other through JV [Vaughters], but we had all already been talking, we had already known each other, we were ready to take the plunge, we were ready to take the risk, whatever direction that would take us,' Danielson said. 'That could have been it for our careers. We weren't a WorldTour team at first. We were joining a young group of guys, leaving seasoned veterans who were winning races, programmes we had all been a part of, just because we believed in this. We believed in the mission.'

They conceded to constant blood monitoring from within their own team, and to criticism from peers who continued to use performance-enhancing drugs. They even subjected themselves to scrutiny from the cantankerous Irish journalist Paul Kimmage, who embedded himself with their team at the 2008 Tour de France, where Vande Velde finished fourth overall.

'To me, it was a huge turning point in the sport when I got a top-five at the Tour without any injections of any kind, whatsoever, due to our no-needles policy,' Vande Velde said. 'And that inspired Bradley Wiggins to come to Garmin, because he saw what I had done, and what we were doing. He went on to win the Tour, and he's a massive advocate for clean sport. And now, you have guys like Andrew Talansky, or Dan Martin, looking up to us. That gives me hope that it is possible. And in all honesty, until I did it, I didn't think it was possible. When I get really down, that's what I tell myself: that it is going to get better in the long term.'

The turning point came in May 2010, when Floyd Landis pulled back the curtain and showed the world what he'd seen during his career, and, specifically, his time on the US Postal Service team.

Landis's admissions launched an investigation, led by federal agent Jeff Novitzky – and a statement from Slipstream Sports, the company that owns the Garmin-Sharp team: 'We expect anyone in our organisation who is contacted by any cycling, anti-doping, or government authority will be open and honest with that authority. In that context, we expect nothing short of 100 per cent truthfulness, whatever that truth is, to the questions they are asked. As long as they express the truth about the past to the appropriate parties, they will continue to have a place in our organisation and we will support them for living up to the promise we gave the world when we founded Slipstream Sports.'

Zabriskie, Danielson, and Vande Velde sat down and, willingly, admitted their wrongdoings to Novitzky in June and July of 2010, immediately after Landis had done the same. They were never subpoenaed. And with the power of a federal perjury charge on his side, Novitzky was able to extract sworn admissions – something even more potent than a positive urine sample.

After US attorney André Birotte, Jr. shuttered the government's case, announcing its closure on a Friday afternoon in February before the 2012 Super Bowl weekend, US Anti-Doping Agency CEO Travis Tygart, who had sat in on early confessions, took up the fight. Eight months later, USADA's reasoned decision was released.

According to their sworn testimony, the last time any of the three Garmin riders had doped was in 2007 – over five years before the USADA report was made public. So why did it take five years, and two investigations, for them to finally publicly acknowledge their drug use?

It's a question I posed to Vaughters, Vande Velde, Danielson, and Zabriskie. Answers varied to a degree, but fell along the same general line of reasoning: change comes from within, and only when there was a critical mass of admissions would it make a difference.

'When we came forward, as a big group, it had an impact on the sport,' Vaughters said. 'If you look back, historically... when Frankie Andreu came forward and admitted to doping [in 2006], what happened? Nothing. When Jörg Jaksche admitted to doping [in 2007], what happened? Nothing. We can come up with 20 stories like this.

'Imagine if, in 2008, we had come forward with this massive admission to doping – and there were plenty of other guys on the team that doped at some point in their career, who weren't named in the USADA report – and the UCI gave everyone a two-year suspension. The team would have ceased to exist,' Vaughters said. 'Lance's PR people would have called it all sour grapes, and the whole thing would have crumbled in an instant. Then fast-forward to 2010, or 2012. Since Slipstream disappeared after all these guys had been suspended, does the USADA case ever happen? Does Jeff [Novitzky] ever go after Lance? Maybe Floyd comes forward, maybe not. Maybe no one backs him up, and the history of the entire thing is entirely and totally different.'

For the riders, it was a matter of actions speaking

louder than words. 'In my mind, in those guys' minds, we'd already made our decision,' Danielson said. 'We were already making progress in the sport, we were already pushing this belief forward.'

Asked if the thought had ever crossed his mind to come forward and admit his transgressions prior to the USADA report, Vande Velde said he felt that the change that was necessary needed to come from within the peloton, not from the UCI or an anti-doping agency.

'I truly believe that the whole mentality, from the inside out, is what truly changes things,' he said. 'Whether it's forced, or just a new generation coming through, or just the belief that you don't need that any more, I believed I was doing a better service by adding to that mentality – that actions were louder than words. And I think that's what's leading the change. I don't think you can argue that. It's not the authorities changing the sport. It's the riders.'

* * *

When the USADA report came out, 'The Garmin Three' suffered the consequences of their actions… sort of. They were stripped of their results during the time that they'd admitted to doping. They were issued six-month suspensions, from September 2012 until March 2013 – essentially the sport's off-season. A suspension for a first offence is usually two years.

They all returned to their positions at Garmin-Sharp shortly after the 2013 season had got under way.

Perhaps the biggest penalties they paid took place in the court of public opinion. Dopers, they were called. Liars. Cheaters. Scumbags. They were told they had no place in the sport, that they should retire, that they should disappear, and make room for the next generation.

And in many ways, these accusations were accurate: Vande Velde, Zabriskie and Danielson had been dopers. They'd been liars, and cheaters. What they had not been, however, was caught red-handed. What they had not been was unrepentant. They'd made the effort to right their wrongs, and they were now being punished, for sins that had, originally, taken place a decade earlier.

'I did find it ironic, and I still do, when we were the ones who took the first step, and were getting our asses kicked by people who hadn't, and we were hanging on the cross, and then we were the ones hanging on the cross again, last year,' Vande Velde told me in June 2013. 'It was hard to take. But I've tried to take myself out of the situation, many times. And I think we continue to inspire, with our training and dedication, and what we do in sport, and that's one of the biggest things. In the bigger picture, I think it's positive.

'It's still happening, and we're still fighting the good fight,' Vande Velde said. 'And we get no credit for that. I'm out there, getting my teeth kicked in, and maybe some of these guys are still doing something. But I'm here, staying my line, being as transparent as possible, and that's all we can really do. It all comes from the mentality of the teams, from the inside out. That's the change. People are pissed off, saying, "Fuck you" [to cheaters], saying, "Get out of the sport." That's the biggest change.'

Asked how he would respond to those who felt they hadn't paid a price, hadn't truly been punished, Vande Velde was reserved in his answer.

'I don't know what to say. I can't win,' he said. 'There are people who don't have the facts right. It wasn't a paid vacation. I didn't go to the London Olympics, and that's a pretty big price – and then Alexandre Vinokourov wins, which was ironic. I didn't get to go to the world championships, which we [Garmin] would have most likely won [the team time trial]. But I can't say anything, right? I'll look like an asshole.'

Danielson was defiant when asked about the price, or lack of price, they'd paid for doping.

'We've been paying prices our whole career,' he said. 'If it's not this, it's something else. It's breaking your shoulder, or it's getting kicked off the Tour team because they don't think you're good enough. There are so many highs and lows with this sport. There's so much shit. Yeah, it sucked last year, to have all those people sending me Twitter messages –

"You should go kill yourself," or, "You're a piece of shit," or, "Look what you are."

'I love to promote cycling, I love spending time with the juniors. That's who I am – I love it. I love talking about cycling with people, and that was the worst thing about it: I felt like people were trying to bat my head out of that, saying, "Well you can't represent cycling. You're a piece of shit." Well, hang on a second, actually, we are the guys who can actually tell these kids, "Hey, cycling is in a good place now. You're in good hands." My whole life is out there for you guys.'

Asked if he was a liar and cheater who profited from his misdeeds, Zabriskie was sheepish.

'For me, it's hard to talk about,' he said. 'I feel bad about it. I feel really bad about it. I kind of always wanted a story to come out about it, and finally it came out. And it had to come out that way. I consider myself an honest person. Honest to a fault, really. What can I say?

'When I was warming up for the California time trial, someone had written "DZ's a rat" on the road,' he continued. 'Seeing my name on the road like that… "Rat" is a mafia term. This isn't the mafia; hopefully no one's gonna get whacked. I told the truth, for myself, and for cycling. And that story gets out there and creates more of that pressure on social media and sponsors and athletes. I don't think anyone wants to see this happen again.'

* * *

Before the 2013 Giro d'Italia had even ended, Di Luca tested positive for EPO and was thrown out of the race. Not much later, his Vini Fantini-Selle Italia team-mate Mauro Santambrogio also tested positive, also for EPO. Suddenly my commentary piece looked prophetic.

'Congratulations,' some folks messaged me. 'You've been vindicated. Di Luca is exactly the unrepentant doper you painted him out to be.'

And, truthfully, I did feel a bit vindicated. Not because Di Luca had proven to be an unrepentant doper – history had already proven this. But because, perhaps, it might lend enough credibility to my editorial piece that those who had bashed it would give it another read, and consider my points in a new light.

As the 2013 season ended, those three Garmin-Sharp riders headed in different directions. Vande Velde's final Tour de France was a disaster, and he abandoned with injuries to his knee, ribs and collarbone. In late August, race organisers presented him on stage with a photo collage after the US Pro Challenge – his final race on US soil.

Danielson finished third overall at that race, two weeks after winning the Tour of Utah – his first still-valid UCI stage-race victory in ten years.

Zabriskie was also at both races, quietly riding in a support role. Asked if his career would continue in

2014, by which time he will have turned 35, Zabriskie was gun-shy.

'I don't know,' he said. 'I just, really, don't know.'

They were all to race together, one last time, at the team time trial world championships in Florence, Italy, in late September, where they were among the top favourites to take the gold medal.

They finished eighth. But what if they had won? Would 'The Garmin Three' deserve to be viewed in a different light than Di Luca? Or Rebellin? Or Valverde? Or anyone else who was caught doping and never admitted to it, never did anything to better the situation?

Clearly, I believe so. And, obviously, so does Vaughters.

'We all know, and knew, that the doping problem was endemic, and sociological, when Zabriskie and Vande Velde showed up in Europe,' Vaughters said. 'This was de facto, this was the way it was done, period. That had existed for years. These guys had to make the choice to disrupt this culture, at their own expense. Valverde has never said he's doped. He's never admitted to his involvement in Operacion Puerto. He's never said he regrets anything. Of course it's different.'

Vande Velde concurred, putting a different spin on it.

'The biggest thing is… afterwards, what have you done to better the sport? Have you mentored kids?

Have you gone to the authorities and explained what you did? Tell me how you're part of the solution.'

Former American pro cyclist Mike Creed, one of the young Americans Vaughters dropped from his spot at Slipstream after he hired Vande Velde, Danielson and Zabriskie – ironic, considering Creed had never touched a needle during his own career – once said something I've never forgotten.

'You're not as good as the best thing you've ever done in your life,' Creed said. 'But you're not as bad as the worst thing either.'

What we all are instead, I believe, is the sum of the moments between those two ends of the morality spectrum. If you accept that the sport of cycling has changed for the better, then you have to credit the people who enacted the change, regardless of the path they took to get there.

And viewed in that light, perhaps only time will tell where 'The Garmin Three' truly belong.

Neal Rogers is editor in chief of *Velo* magazine and *VeloNews.com*. An interest in all things rock 'n' roll led him into music journalism while attending UC Santa Cruz, on the central coast of California. After several post-grad years spent waiting tables, surfing, and mountain biking, he moved to San Francisco, working as a bike messenger, and at a software startup. He moved to Boulder, Colorado, in 2001, taking an editorial internship at *VeloNews*. He never left. When not travelling the world covering races, he can be found riding his bike, skiing, or attending a concert.

2

British, but having grown up in Kenya and South Africa.

Quiet and well-mannered, yet monstrously fast on a bike.

Chris Froome is a mixture of different things in so many ways: a true one-off.

But, **Ned Boulting** asks, who is the 2013 Tour champion really?

THE INDIVISIBLE MAN

BY NED BOULTING

'Krees-toff-air-From!'

Daniel Mangeas, the straw-haired legend, the tall and loping voice of the Tour, his lips brushing the foam pop shield of his microphone, never deviated once from his pronunciation. Four syllables, equally stressed, but with a slight downturn at the end, the 'From!' marking an emphatic full-stop.

Deuxième du Tour de France en 2012, vainqueur du Tour de Romandie, vainqueur du Critérium International, vainqueur du Critérium du Dauphiné, et le Maillot Jaune du Tour de France… Krees-toff-air-From!'

And then he'd pause to implore the waiting, and largely indifferent, hordes to purchase a certain washing-powder tablet – a request which they almost certainly ignored. In fact, it wasn't just detergent that was proving hard to sell.

It was Chris Froome himself.

* * *

A little honesty: I was late delivering this chapter.

If it hadn't been for the fact that I like Ellis and Lionel a great deal, and that their project (this book) is admirable, their hard work indisputable and their loyalty exceptional, I might quietly have made the commission go away. But a promise is a promise, and I had assured them that I would deliver a chapter about Chris Froome, however late. For the lateness, I apologise.

It wasn't going to be about his performance on a bike; Heaven knows there's been enough written about that. Nor was it intended as a biography; those tidbits of an African childhood have been well aired by now. I wanted instead to lift the curtain a little on the Chris Froome with whom I had daily contact during the month of July, to glimpse fleetingly behind the mask of the man who won the Tour.

This was not going to be easy. I've had plenty of experience of talking to Froome, both on and off the record, but have always been left with the same feeling: a slight, unaccountable, nagging frustration. A sense of not quite getting to the nub of the matter.

One more attempt, then: a girding of the journalistic loins, a heaving into sight of my target. Would I finally 'get' Froome?

* * *

I have made Froome-bothering something of a profession. I remember well the sudden realisation,

during the 2008 Tour de France, that there was a
'bona fide' Briton in the peloton who absolutely
nobody had heard of. I was duly dispatched to go
and meet the kid. I looked up his hotel details and,
together with my colleague – the estimable Matt
Rendell – we loaded the car with camera equipment,
and went off in search of our prey.

The race was trundling out of Brittany and starting to unwind into long, straight sections bound for
the Massif Central. The sun had broken through as
we'd left behind us the Atlantic drizzle of the *Grand
Départ*. Team Barloworld had lucked out with this
hotel: a sweet *auberge* with a garden and a terrace,
soft upholstery and an air of quiet relaxation. Riders
and staff slouched around the foyer, some conducted muted post-breakfast telephone conversations
with loved ones, others stared blankly into space,
visualising the unimaginable rigours of the day that
lay ahead of them.

Where to begin? We recognised no one. We
began to do the thing that so often we resort to on
the Tour: winging it. The first person we accosted,
in the fond supposition that he might be the *directeur
sportif* on a team that boasted almost nobody of any
note, turned out instead to be their Italian bus driver,
who confessed to having no idea which one of the
riders he drove around France was Chris Froome.
'Kreesa Fromm?' A shrug. A smile. 'No.'

Then, suddenly, a rider appeared – a familiar face.

The problem was now one of diplomacy. How best to get the information we wanted without making it obvious that we had no interest in actually talking to Baden Cooke himself. Besides, he looked ravaged; gaunt, grey, thin. Unwell. My surprise at finding him riding for such a minor team (he had, after all, won the green jersey in 2003) was matched only by my surprise at seeing Matt Rendell completely fail to recognise him. Matt never failed to recognise anyone.

'Sorry, I didn't catch your name...' Matt beamed at him, and stretched out his hand in greeting.

'Matt,' I intervened hastily. 'It's Baden Cooke.'

'Christ.' Matt was mortified by his faux pas. 'Baden. Bloody hell. Sorry.'

There was something about Barloworld that didn't feel right. They were rudderless from the start, their Tour fatally undermined when their leader, Mauricio Soler, the Colombian 'king of the mountains' from 2007, fractured his wrist in a fall on stage one, and climbed off four days later.

But it went deeper than that: they looked cobbled together. A clutch of South Africans mixing it with a smattering of South Americans, Spaniards and Australians. Sometimes, of course, this kind of constellation works. Other times, on other teams, it just looks like a bunch of riders who didn't know each other, but whose contracts had one common thread: affordability. Just at the point at which Team Sky was first being dreamed up, Barloworld were busily providing the counterpoint: the way not to do it.

Eventually – and I forget how many more blind alleys we had to run through to reach our destination – I came face to face with Chris Froome.

He ghosted into a reception area strewn with sofas – his arrival unheralded, his introductions meek. He struck me as a little awkward and very shy: young, and immensely, incalculably, irredeemably out of place. This, I calculated in a split second, was no bike rider. This was a schoolboy, a choirboy, a reluctant boy scout, with all the badges for Plant Identification, and none for Physical Prowess. This was the pale, asthmatic (there is no evidence to suggest he has asthma) kid who was excused from PE on the grounds of a persistent cold. This was the kid who'd forgotten his gym kit (there is no evidence to prove that he has ever forgotten his gym kit). Not – quite emphatically not – a future winner of the Tour de France.

Talking to him with the camera rolling was as affably unremarkable as talking to him without the camera rolling. Each phrase, neatly wrapped in that softest of soft Anglo-Southern-African sing-song, was suffused with the intent to cause no harm, primarily to himself, but equally to his team and to others. He wanted to tread a kindly path into whichever course his future might explore. I tuned out after the first few banalities about his British ancestry, and his limited ambitions on this sudden and unexpected elevation to the status of Grand Tour rider.

Instead, I became fascinated by his collar.

I have an eye for the un-ironed, born from my own personal shortcomings. It struck me straight off that Chris Froome had hastily pulled a Barloworld regulation polo shirt from his suitcase (not a meta-phorical 'suitcase of courage', but an actual 'suitcase of clothes'), and come down to do the interview, hoping to do the right thing by his team management and sponsors. The result, on TV, was a collar so wrin-kled that the word 'Barloworld' had been reduced to a shortened and therefore baffling 'Browrd'.

We shook hands. He was charming. He was 23. And there I left him. In the greater scheme of things, and in this particular Tour, he was of little further importance. I did not realise, at the time, that he had lost his mother, the woman who had raised him alone after her separation from his father, a matter of weeks before the race. I wish I had known. I would have paid more attention.

* * *

We did meet again, once, on that Tour.

Barloworld continued, in largely unexpected ways, to create extraordinary headlines. After Soler's abandon, the next calamity, in this particular CERA-('second-generation EPO') sodden race, was the police raid on their hotel after stage ten. That did for Moisés Dueñas. Then they lost two more the next day in a wildly unlikely racing incident. Robbie Hunter, the belligerent sprinter, who had been instrumental in Froome's early career, was beside himself with fury. Most of this fury, when I questioned Hunter at the finish line, he decided to focus on me.

A week later, Froome's young friend, John Lee Augustyn, opted famously to tumble down the side of an Alp, aping the great heroes of Pathé footage from yesteryear. He tried to scramble up the near vertical scree slope, and for a second looked like he'd lose his footing entirely and tumble into the abyss. Sometimes, even now, the memory of this jolts me awake in the middle of the night. Not because of that, though. It's Robbie Hunter who scares me.

I was interviewing Froome about the incident at the end of the stage, outside the seriously underpopulated Barloworld bus (only four of that team made it to Paris), when I became aware that there was a madman pressing his face against the tinted glass, and gesturing that he would like to have my throat cut. This distracting apparition was Robbie Hunter. I quite lost my thread, and failed to listen as I should have done to the words of my young interviewee.

To this day, I have no idea why he wanted me dead. But Hunter and I have never spoken since. Nor have I happened across Soler, Augustyn, Cooke, nor Dueñas.

Not the case with Froome, though. He, as it happened, was the one. The One.

* * *

He joined Sky, of course.

One dank Blackpool morning in the autumn of
2009, at the start of stage four of the Tour of Britain, Dave Brailsford, clad in his red, white and blue
GB tracksuit with its discreet Sky logo sewn to his
breast, was doing the rounds.

The race was peppered with riders he had
either already signed up, wooed, courted or intended
to lure. There was Edvald Boasson Hagen, in the
acid yellow of HTC-Columbia, Ian Stannard, riding
for Italian outfit ISD, Ben Swift looking thoroughly
lost in Katusha's colours, Chris Sutton in his Garmin
argyle; all these and more. He stopped for a long
chat with Ag2r's Nicolas Roche (a move that never
happened), and then he set up shop outside the Barloworld bus.

Here he had rich pickings. It was always clear
that Geraint Thomas would be a prized asset, and
that there would be a role for the gnarly expertise
of Steve Cummings. But Froome? There was almost
a sense of box-ticking duty about his signing. He
was, after all, sort of British. Brailsford spent little
time with him that morning in Blackpool; a cursory
checking-up on details, the practicalities of making
the switch. Had he got his invitation to the team's
induction meeting in November? He was perhaps
one of the last names on the list.

There had been the minutest of glimpses on that 2008 Tour de France of his ability to survive in the GC group on climbs. Every now and again, his tall, ungainly form would be glimpsed near the front of the race as it powered up the lower slopes. Then he would fall away. Still, that was enough, coupled with the facts of his nationality and his (relatively) meagre salary demands, to seal the deal.

Perhaps he fell into the category of 'might as well have him'. At times, Brailsford's recruitment policy has been a little scattergun. He has brought in riders because they've got something about them, no more than that. How they might best be used? That'll come out in the wash. But in Froome's case, expectations were not high.

I saw him again in the spring of the following year – in 2010. The night before, I had been covering a football match in Turin for ITV. I hired a car, and drove down to Quarrata to see Chris Froome. He was living alone in Pete Kennaugh's tiny apartment in town.

We sat on the cool stone floor, as he drank some herbal tea. He'd been training alone, and brutally hard, for weeks. Six, seven-hour rides, and then back home, alone, to feast on his lunch: an apple. The weight, not that he had much to start with, was falling off him.

That day, three years ago, he told me that he wanted to become a GC rider. I was surprised by how confident he seemed. He understood that he would be in Bradley Wiggins's shadow, but he stated his ambition clearly. He wanted to compete for the biggest prize in the sport, and he thought he would one day be good enough.

I wished him well, and left him to it. He struck me as lonely, perhaps misguided. I still had in mind the boy with the wrinkly collar.

* * *

These snapshots, then, constitute a cipher; a code from which to unpick the hidden Froome, the one that existed before the spotlight turned on him.

His breakthrough moments have been well documented. They read like a Wikipedia entry: the 2011 Vuelta a España, with his blistering time trial, his twin-turbo duet with Wiggins on the long-form climbs, his acceleration on the Angliru, and his refusal to be beaten by Juan José Cobo on the slopes of Peña Cabarga.

The bickering has been equally well exposed. The 2012 Tour, with its echoes of Bernard Hinault and Greg LeMond, was every bit as acrimonious, it seems, as we might have imagined, looking on from a distance. Even in Paris – even as the sun was setting on Wiggins's triumphant procession – one member of Sky's management team still had steam coming out of his ears over Froome's perceived lack of loyalty.

'He's an Afrikaaner, Ned,' I was told, erroneously. 'You can't trust them.'

So, in the summer of 2013, as we headed for the start line in Corsica, we all knew the story – the building blocks of a career in a hurry: the Kenyan boyhood, the long, long rides with David Kinjah, the tumble he took at the Commonwealth Games, his battle with the water-borne parasite bilharzia, his ungainliness, his unpredictability, his instinct, the sudden rise in his fortunes. But was it a story we would be able to embrace?

He and I happened to be on the same flight from Nice to Figari, queuing at check-in behind Peter Sagan and Roman Kreuziger. No one was paying much attention to the odds-on favourite to win the Tour de France. He might as well have been invisible. In a few weeks, that would surely change forever.

'What've you been up to for the last few weeks, Chris?'

'Just at home, training.'

'Hard? Or tapering? Resting up?'

'Pretty hard actually.' Then a smile. 'In fact, I've been timing my rides up the Col de la Madone. I've been smashing Armstrong's record.'

At the time, he asked me to keep that to myself, perhaps correctly guessing that the Twitterati doping sleuths would be all over that particular nugget. But he couldn't hide his delight in knowing how fast he was. How fast we would be.

***

'Definitely.'

He has a habit, Chris Froome, of nodding and smiling in agreement with the assertion, or the tone, of the opening question. I'd remembered that from our very first meeting, in the crumpled nylon weave of Barloworld, and now he still exhibited the same tics, albeit these days smoothly kitted out by Rapha.

'Definitely.'

I suspect it's just in his nature: a consensus kind of man.

'A hundred per cent.'

From the moment he assumed the race lead, at Ax-3 Domaines, I was, frankly, in pest mode. I had a contractual obligation, and so did he. His patience with the media was, at times, laudable, surprising, ill-advised, dignified, perplexing. Every day I would be second in line, getting to him after French TV had stuck an earpiece in his lughole and cajoled him into reliving every last pedal turn of the stage. And, after me, he was paraded through the massed ranks of hacks. Radio was the most aggressive, thrusting clusters of primary coloured microphones of various nationalities under his nose, and talking doping. There was other stuff on their agenda, occasionally, but mostly it was doping.

'I know that what I am doing is a hundred per-cent clean.' He would tell them this over and over

again. Proving a negative was like trying to catch an
eel with your bare hands.

He would, on occasions, take a breather, ac-
companied by Dario Cioni, the former rider turned
PR chap for Sky, walking alongside him, holding an
umbrella, cracking open a can of drink, clutching a
cuddly lion and handing him a Tupperware box containing what looked like coronation chicken. Hiding
then, behind the caravan in which the podium girls
got made up, he'd greedily load up a few desperate
forkfuls of protein before returning to the fray.

On the first rest day, Sky had been billeted near
the beach at La Baule. After two or three days of
dealing with the welter of doping questions, an
atmosphere of buckets, spades and sandcastles
might have invited the Tour's media masses to kindly
move on and indulge in a bit of holiday bonhomie by
talking about the race.

Not a bit of it. Paul Kimmage, flanked by his
documentary crew, was typically determined in his
questioning. At the 'top table', Froome sat centre
stage, with Richie Porte, wrinkling his nose at the
tone of some of the enquiries, to his left. Froome
was inscrutable, answering with the same slow
emphasis, but sometimes gilded with the slightest
hint of exasperation. Only once, and for the
first time on the Tour, did his attitude veer into
bullishness. He was asked by Kimmage about Sky's
misguided appointment of the Belgian doctor Geert

Leinders – a story that had been hard currency almost a year previously, but now seemed curiously off-kilter. And then he was asked by a Scandinavian voice, emerging out of the air–conditioned gloom of the subterranean press conference room, 'How can you explain that your performances against former champions are so dominant?' He meant Cadel Evans and Andy Schleck, perhaps. But mostly he meant Alberto Contador.

Froome answered in generalities, and placed the microphone on the table. Then, abruptly, he picked it back up again. 'Perhaps you might want to ask them why it is that they are not performing to the same standards that they used to.'

It was the first time he had tried to direct the argument elsewhere. The subtext? Leave me alone.

He then submitted himself to a separate grilling in French (a language he is only just becoming competent in) at the hands of those infamous radio reporters and web-content networks. They're the cameramen who double-up as journalists, holding a microphone and trying to look through a viewfinder at the same time. Experience teaches riders to be wary of these sometimes roguish operators; you never know what you are going to get. Although, by now, Chris Froome could have had a fair guess.

'C'est bien simple. Beaucoup de travail. Beaucoup d'entraînement.'

That was the sweat-inducing gist of it, squinting into a battery of camera lights.

'*Je sais que je suis propre.*'

In another corner of the room, Richie Porte was holding court, telling all and sundry that they might like to go beat up on someone else for a change. I was reminded of how close the two men were.

Back in the spring, I had returned from the Critérium International with them on the same tiny aeroplane from Ajaccio to Nice. They had finished the race in an unassailable one-two.

'Why don't people like Sky?' Porte had asked me. 'What can we do about it?'

Next to him, taciturn, wrapped up in thoughts of his own, Froome had unpacked a copy of *The Secret Race* by Tyler Hamilton and had started to read. As we got off the plane, I asked him about it.

'Just unbelievable, what they got up to,' he said. 'Unimaginable.'

Then they made their way through arrivals, to where Michelle Cound, Froome's fiancée, was waiting to pick them up. That was back in March.

This was the heat of July.

* * *

As Chris Froome did battle with Movistar and Saxo-Tinkov and the rest of them, so my job started to fall into a routine. It was the same pattern that had first, and remarkably, been established the previous year on the Planche des Belles Filles. It involved the sudden absorption of all my efforts on the Tour into one story: a British race leader. That fact altered everything.

In 2012, when Wiggins first assumed the lead, such an elevated status was, of course, unprecedented. There was no template for me to follow, and I had to change entirely the nature of what I did on the Tour; all that I had hitherto thought the race was about. Cavendish's series of stage wins aside, I was unused to British interest at the heart of the race. In fact, all through the latter Armstrong years, over the speed bumps of Landis, Rasmussen, Contador, Evans and Sastre, we had viewed our role at ITV as reluctant invitees to someone else's party, standing in the corner, nursing a gin and tonic, making wry observations about all the other guests to anyone who cared to listen. We certainly weren't used to being dragged onto the dance floor and forced to take centre stage. This was thoroughly un-British; much more fun, really, to snipe from the sidelines.

It's like this: the Tour affords special access to the national broadcaster of the race leader. You get to go where you are normally not allowed, behind the podium, where the riders first appear, chaperoned through the chaos of the finish line into the slightly more refined chaos of the protocol. The price you have to pay? Best behaviour.

At least, those rules certainly applied to us. Wiggins had driven the organisation mad with his unpredictable attitude to his media obligations; sometimes charming, sometimes hilarious, and at other times curt, foul-mouthed or simply absent. One particular favourite ruse of his was to disappear into the anti-doping caravan before he had dealt with the waiting broadcasters. The onerous obligation to produce urine from a dehydrated metabolism in sufficient quantities to satisfy the men in white coats was usually something the wearer of the yellow jersey saved till last.

Through successive TV interviews, he'd be gulping down sugary drinks in such volume that, by the time he was ready to go, he was ready to go. Except, midway through the Tour, Bradley Wiggins figured out that if he went straight for the 'piss wagon' and sat it out, then by the time he finally emerged, blinking into the late afternoon sunlight, most of the assembled TV crews would have given up and gone home.

'Why does he do this?' the French TV floor manager, Pablo, asked, genuinely perplexed at such pranks.

'I don't know,' I told him.

Actually, I did know. I just pretended I didn't.

'You have to admit, it's quite clever,' I grinned at him.

Pablo shrugged and walked off in search of

Thomas Voeckler, or someone more compliant.

With Froome, it was different. There was no subterfuge, no cheekiness, no drop of the shoulder nor swerving of obligations. It didn't make him any more charismatic, any more adored or fawned over, or any more the focus for fascination. But it did make him respected, liked even, by an increasingly weary press pack. Even Christian Prudhomme fell under his subtle spell, professing that he found Froome 'very elegant in his way of speaking, with a sweet voice'. Then, rather fulsomely, he added that he thought Froome's eyes were 'very expressive'.

Throughout the race, Froome remained admirably tolerant, almost as a matter of principle; perhaps even as a point of pride, or difference to his predecessor. The strongest expression of his desire to be anywhere else other than standing around answering the same unanswerable question for the 20th time that day would take the form of a half step to the left and a polite grimace if he felt that time was up. Once, when a confusion of microphones was thrust a little too forcibly under his mouth, he took a visible step back. That was as brattish as he got.

I asked him, as he sat down at nine o'clock one evening to a long chat for Sky News, how many interviews he'd done that day. It was a throwaway question, really, which I hadn't expected him to take seriously. I thought he'd just roll his eyes heavenwards and say, 'Too many.' Instead, he gazed into the middle distance, his lips silently moving as he counted. After what seemed like an eternity, he answered.

'Thirty eight.' Then he turned towards his questioner to do his 39th, and final, interview of the day.

* * *

But how was it all playing back home? What net return was Chris Froome and his expensively assembled sponsors' brand yielding in the UK market? Did the people like him? Was he the new Wiggo? Were we complicit in selling Froome to willing buyers?

It was hard to measure, but in a summer that was composed of a string of unusually hot and sunny evenings (a toxic combination for TV ratings) and unheralded British success on the manicured green lawns of Wimbledon, the Tour seemed not to be consuming the public imagination with the same sudden vigour as it had done the previous year. With Wiggins, in 2012, it had been quantifiable: I measured the meteoric impact of his impending win in phone calls from radio stations.

'Ned, would you be available to talk on our breakfast show?' 'Could you do the Drivetime programme tomorrow?'

As that Tour ground towards a conclusion, so my phone became busier and busier. Britain, or at least that bit of it populated by radio producers, suddenly discovered an unquenchable thirst for the Tour de

France, and specifically for its lank-haired, sweary hero.

But not this year. Save for the odd (and it was invariably odd) chat with Alan Brazil on TalkSport, my phone stayed silent. One year on, a different rider, a different race. Besides, as British cycling fans, our constituents had been there, done that and worn the replica yellow jersey.

I bumped into David Walsh. He'd spent the whole Tour sharing accommodation and team cars with the Sky personnel. He had been watching Froome at first hand. We talked about how he came across, how the story was playing out, how he'd adapted to the intensity of his new-found status.

'The thing is,' Walsh said, 'the public are no mugs. Nobody really buys the British thing, not even Chris. And it's such a shame – a missed opportunity. If he'd only come to the Tour with a Kenyan racing licence, as the first African to win, then what a story! Then we'd have something we could truly embrace – a story we could all get behind.'

As we talked, I watched Froome signing autographs. His shades were on, but he was smiling courteously.

* * *

The race ground on. There were signs of weakness, but not many. The crosswinds threatened briefly to blow the race apart on the road to Saint-Pourçain-sur-Sioule: that day Froome lost half of the time he'd made on Contador in the individual time trial. With uncomfortable timing (at least from his perspective), it was also the day we had agreed with Froome's Sky PR management that we would be granted some special access. Our cameras picked him up and followed him through an evening's routine, from the moment he climbed into his air-conditioned Jaguar and clunked the door shut on all the madness. In the midst of this calm, he suddenly found the blank eye of our cameraman's lens pointing at him, barely two feet from where he now sat on the rear passenger seat. A lesser man might have reacted differently, perhaps violently differently. Froome, though, opening his Tupperware box of chicken, simply asked Dario, 'How far to the hotel?'

'Forty-five minutes.'

Froome sighed. The stage had finished over an hour and a half ago, and he was still a long way from getting a shower.

Perhaps that was it. Maybe that was the problem. Never mind the slightly dubious nature of his British-ness; perhaps it was simply his love of Tupperware. Maybe we demand more from our athletes than the simple desire to neither offend, nor stir up controversy. We want them to lose it, and the more publicly, the better: the Armstrong tirade at Paul Kimmage, Cadel Evans head-butting a cameraman, Cavendish turning the air blue, Wiggins being four-lettered. It's what TV lives for, and, if we're honest, what we tune in for. That's why we place athletes under such scrutiny; on occasion it is a provocation. A dirty business, I couldn't help feeling.

But the Faustian pact had been struck, and uncomfortable though we all were with the process (we skirted him as much as we could and tried to apply discretion), ITV would get its pound of flesh.

He arrived back at their tiny little two-star hotel far too late for a massage before his dinner. So, after a shower, and a bite to eat, and after conducting a breathtakingly ill-informed television interview (and I know all about them!) for his sponsors, only then did he head for a rub-down. It was almost dark outside. The day had been long for all concerned, and showed no signs of ending any time soon.

We struck a compromise, which suited all parties. We decided to cheat.

We filmed Froome going into the room, and then, straight away, we filmed him 'leaving', even though he hadn't actually had a massage. That way, after grabbing a minute's worth of footage of him actually being kneaded, we could bid our farewells and leave him in peace without the need for us to hang around in the corridor for an hour to get a shot of him on the way out.

As we prepared this dishonest little sequence, Chris Froome – because he is a fundamentally accommodating individual and aims to please – decided to embroider his part, and to add to the authenticity of the shot. This meant that as he came out of the room, right on cue, he turned rather woodenly to the camera and said, 'Ah – that feels much better.' It wasn't going to win him a Bafta.

Then he smartly turned and started to walk away from the camera and down the corridor. At that precise moment, a door opened in front of him, and Alberto Contador, the man who lay second in the Tour de France, suddenly appeared walking briskly towards him. The two men met, and, vaguely aware of the presence of the camera, exchanged rather awkward pleasantries. Then they went their separate ways. It was a very 'cycling' moment – the kind of chance encounter in a crappy two-star hotel between two star riders which could only happen on the Tour.

We stopped filming. Chris Froome walked back towards us, grinning broadly.

'You couldn't make it up.'

Unfortunately, though, in a way, we had. That's telly for you, I'm afraid. Don't trust it.

* * *

On Mont Ventoux, I had no telly. This was the realisation that struck me as I took up my position on the finish line just as the peloton was about to hit the foot of the climb. I had no telly, and no way of seeing the defining day unfold. Just as I realised the gravity of my situation, Dave Brailsford came loping down the road towards me.

'Is there a telly anywhere?' he enquired.

'I've got the same issue, Dave,' I told him. 'No.'

'There's one in the team car. You can join me there if you want.'

And so it was that I watched the race-winning move unfold alongside Brailsford in the front seats of a Jaguar, with Chris Haynes (Sky's PR manager), Dario Cioni and David Walsh scrunched up along the rear passenger seats behind. From a telly built into the dashboard, France Sport TV's commentators were starting to go through their gears, just as the riders were doing the same.

Omega Pharma-Quick Step had joined the front of the peloton, mysteriously helping to catch a breakaway group containing their own Sylvain Chavanel. Brailsford was onto that tactic straight away.

'So, they'll be wanting us to help lead out Cav on the Champs-Elysées then!'

I wasn't sure if he was joking. I'm still not certain.

Then, later, Froome attacked. Brailsford dropped his BlackBerry. 'Go on Froomey! Go on Froome Dog!'

It amused me, and surprised me, to witness this. Firstly to see him so animated. I remember attempting a spontaneous and regrettable man-hug with Dave Brailsford in Chartres on the day that Wiggins clinched the 2012 Tour, only to be told, 'You know me – I'm a boring bastard. I don't do excited.'

But also, I was taken aback to hear him use the term 'Froome Dog'. It's never been a comfortable fit, as far as I am concerned – a nickname born of artifice and irony, and out of the need to have a nickname. Like 'Va Va Froome', it was not ever going to go viral. Not properly.

But here was Dave Brailsford, lifted half out of his expensive leather car seat with the sheer fun of it, the thrill, the fandom, almost. And at the very same moment as we were all thinking, 'Why's he gone so early?' he slapped his palm against his forehead and swore. 'Bloody hell, Froomey. Why've you gone so bloody early?'

'You've got a racing animal, there, Dave,' Walsh chipped in from the back of the car. 'He can't help himself.'

'Don't I know it.' Brailsford's BlackBerry chirruped with an incoming text. James Murdoch, it seemed, was watching the race, somewhere in the world.

Later that day, after the two-armed salute on top of Mont Ventoux, in yellow, on the 100th Tour, on Bastille Day, and after oxygen had been rushed to his side, Chris Froome spoke to us as he went diligently through his warm-down on the rollers. By now, we had a routine. Once he'd done a few minutes of more intense spinning, he eased off the cadence, took a swig of water, and, with a pleasant smile, beckoned us near.

I can't remember what it was that I put to him exactly, but I found myself pointing at the view behind him. The mountain road, snaking away to the south, past the Tom Simpson memorial, before disappearing eventually into the forest of the lower slopes. And beyond that, the flatlands of the south, dipping down all the way to the Côte d'Azur, and across the sea, to Corsica. I think I was vaguely alluding to the grandeur of it all.

He paused, and, still turning the pedals, looked over his right shoulder at the view, as if taking it all in for the first time.

'Gosh,' he said. 'Look at it.'

* * *

The setting for the final, processional stage into Paris was equally magnificent. Having spent the night in Annecy, and while the rest of the Tour thundered up the motorway to the capital city (and I was struck, not for the first time, by how, past midnight, Tour de France vehicles constitute almost all the traffic on the autoroute), the riders flew up the following morning. On landing they were driven to their team buses parked outside the Palace of Versailles, where they had a three or four-hour wait until the late-afternoon stage start. With the evening finish on the Champs-Elysées, the whole day had a jet-lagged feel to it.

We had two riders to interview. One was Mark Cavendish, for whom we waited for hours (Rob Hayles will testify to this; he waited alongside me) while he came and went, in and out of his team bus, adjusting bits of kit, trying on a new pair of shoes, getting his mechanics to change the pedals, and then change them back.

But a more sizeable chunk of British support had gathered by the Team Sky bus to wait for the second name on our list. They were there for Chris Froome, and so were we. We filmed an interview, our penultimate interview of a long summer, with him perched on a car bonnet, in front of a crowd of Union Jacks and replica kits and smiling faces, exuding goodwill in his direction.

Finally, finally, we could both relax, a little.

'What did you eat last night?'

'Hamburger and chips.'

'How much do you weigh this morning?'

For the first time, a genuine, spontaneous smile. Chris Froome threw his head back and laughed, properly, not out of politeness.

'About a kilo more than this time yesterday.'

'Have you written a speech?'

'I have a few ideas, yes.'

I thanked him for a month of athlete/reporter

symbiosis. I thought he deserved a little apprecia-
tion. Then, with a smile and a nod to the crowds, he
turned and left for the shade of the team bus. They
cheered, and a small chant of 'Froomey!' broke out.

It faded, as the hydraulic door swung closed.

* * *

A few hours later, the sun dipped, and the race
ended. Now, set against that familiar backdrop, but
floodlit this time, and from my standing perspective
just to the side, silhouetted against his own grainy
image projected onto a huge screen, Chris Froome
took to the top step of the podium, one higher
than that uncomfortable second place of 2012. He
unfolded his notes.

There were to be no jokes, no references to
raffles. Just a well-wrought phrase about his own
propriety.

That, and an understated, and exceptionally rare,
nod to his departed mother. And again I was reminded of young Chris Froome, the first time I met him,
on his first Tour de France.

* * *

And that's where I leave him now: a slightly
uncertain-looking figure, talking with disarming shy-
ness into a microphone, into the night sky, towards

Paris. The winner of the 100th Tour de France is as unlikely a hero as any who have gone before him.

The boy from nowhere, meekly setting about his work, hunched over a bike, head nodding; an assuming, well-bred beast. He may have the gaze of an accountant, and the manners of a priest, but he is a racer, pure and simple, unquenchable in his thirst, his ambition, curious only to satisfy one particular, driven enquiry. How good can he be?

Will Chris Froome be great? Is he already great? Who is he, really?

Look straight at him for the answer. Look carefully. It's there, somewhere. But I'm damned if I can find it.

Ned Boulting has now covered 11 Tours de France for ITV. 'Bloody hell. That's nearly a whole year of them.' He is also the author of *How I Won the Yellow Jumper* and *On the Road Bike: The Search For a Nation's Cycling Soul*.

3

No one would argue that a slow march towards a dope-free sport isn't a good thing.

There is already evidence that the clean-up is affecting not just the level of performances riders are able to produce but the frequency with which they can attain those heights.

Kenny Pryde asks whether the sport's shift away from a reliance on doping and recovery products means riders will be unable to stay at the top of their game for as long as their predecessors.

TWO-BOB ROCKETS

BY KENNY PRYDE

'The light that burns twice as bright burns half as long, and you have burned so very, very brightly, Roy. Look at you.'

Eldon Tyrell to android Roy Batty
Blade Runner, 1982

Let us imagine we are set to enjoy a few years of bike racing during which doping will not overshadow racing. Once the last elements of 'Generation EPO' have either 'fessed up or kept their mouths shut and slipped away, it's reasonable to assume that the doping 'shocks' will stop hogging headlines. At that point, maybe we'll be able to pause, take stock and consider what this 'new' cycling is.

Note, please, that there's no suggestion here that we are witnessing a totally clean cycling – a kind of two-wheeled sporting utopia.

When transnational sport, global media and big money are involved, such a position will always be untenable, but, by general consent, inside the peloton, things are much better than they were.

So let us assume that we are currently witnessing UCI WorldTour racing that is less medically-assisted than before – possibly even than ever before. No one is under any illusions that there aren't still riders using performance-enhancing products to cheat, and using technologies and strategies that are on the limit of what is permissible, ethical and in the spirit of the sport. But it's credible to believe that we are enjoying some bike racing wherein doping using cocktails of various steroids, hormones and cortisone is at its lowest level since Amgen's synthetic EPO was unleashed on the sporting world in the early 1990s.

When Generation EPO (or should that be Generation Haemo?) first drew breath, it should have been clear enough. There were magnificent sights and staggering feats to behold. In Robert Millar's memorable phrase that few grasped at the time, this was the era of 'the 80-kilogram climber' when, almost overnight, 'guys who couldn't climb a railway bridge were sailing past me going up climbs, sitting down, in the big ring'. Funny that everyone 'gets' it now, but somehow, in the 1990s, it passed the sports administrators, sponsors and the race organisers by. Many journalists assumed that heart-rate monitors were the secret – and in any case, the law of *omertà* was observed on both sides of the media fence.

But we digress. That era has been consigned to a history that is still being written, and it's heavy with footnotes. Doping stories still leak out, but with less and less impact, to less and less interest as the sins of the past are buried in a bloody pit. Collectively, there's little stomach for untangling the ethical, legal and sporting mess that generation left as a legacy. All we're left with are a few shrivelled heads on spikes at the city gates to discourage others. Well, it's some kind of closure...

So, as we emerge coughing and spluttering out of the smoke from the bonfire of the *palmarès*, what is this brave new world we are confronted by? Crudely, if riders aren't charged to the gills on hormones, red blood cells and cortisone, what sort of racing are we witnessing now and what can we expect in the future? If these products had such profound physiological effects on riders, now that they no longer have those chemical crutches, logically things have had to change.

Now that the major war on PEDs has been won (more or less), and we're left tidying up pockets of resistance, there's the inevitable collateral 'damage' to deal with. The aftermath. What will inevitably be lost is the 'old' style of racing – the success of buccaneering solo attacks from general classification contenders, together with the near impossibility of riders dominating the sport for years. The long-distance attacks of Claudio Chiappucci and Marco Pantani won't be happening again any time soon. The audiences who were thrilled and inspired by those sorts of exploits will have to get used to seeing different styles of racing. It's not a transition that has been met with universal approval or understanding. We've all heard the comments from those watching Grand Tours: 'Why don't riders attack any more? Why do riders wait till the last climb or the final kilometres to attack?'

Where are the 'Pirates'? The 'Devils'? We won't be seeing riders winning five Tours on the trot (far less seven) any more. And why?

There are several reasons, ranging from sponsorship money, physiology, sports science, nutrition, improved anti-doping strategies and a change in the culture of younger riders. Doping was never about 'evil', or about some bad apples spoiling an otherwise organic barrel of goodness. There are a near infinite number of factors influencing doping practices in sport, so to single out 'key' figures and calling them evil sociopaths is simplistic to the point of idiocy.

In any case, one change in the cultural landscape that hasn't been as high in explanations about the changes wrought by a 'doping-lite' culture is the new focus and determination required to be a Grand Tour contender.

If you are going to win a Grand Tour these days, more than ever, you need a level of discipline and mental toughness that is simply unsustainable over long periods. Nobody is pretending that the best dopers didn't have discipline, but to race a Grand

Tour for the general classification clean – particularly in the current McCarthyite witch-trial ambiance of the Tour – takes something extra again.

The psychological crutch and physiological certainties offered by blood doping and associated practices have gone. Riders and teams are under much more scrutiny from both the media and anti-doping organisations than ever before. Doping, always risky even in the good old days, is less of an option than ever.

David Millar, speaking to me in 2012, observed that the days when there were small groups of people within teams who were still involved in, for want of any better expression, 'the bad stuff', were gone.

'That doesn't exist any more. If you are doing the bad stuff now, you have to be so incredibly secret about it, it's like the dark arts. To get away with it, you are talking about incredibly advanced doping, a lot of money and an amazing level of logistics. You are talking about real criminality and a really sophisticated entourage; it's not something you can simply 'slip into' – certainly not in terms of top-end, sophisticated doping. It does happen, still, but it's such a different sport now.'

That phrase from Millar – 'It's such a different sport now' – is worth looking at because, on one level, the Grand Tours still last three brutal weeks and the spring Classics are still 250 kilometres long. The most obvious difference is in the reduction of

sophisticated and systemic doping. But the sport is
also being detoxed of its reliance on injected and
infused medications. A *soigneur* is no longer able
to hook a rider up to a bag of 'recovery' product,
else he, the team and the rider face heavy sanction.
It's a long way from blood bags dangling from coat
hangers in hotel rooms.

Cast your mind back to the days before Generation EPO. Recall, if you will, the number of times
you heard the phrase 'recovery', or noticed this subject being raised in interviews, or in those infrequent
discussions about training. Anecdotally, I'd say that
'recovery' wasn't really a hot topic – not when there
was information about the precise duration of inter-
val training to be prised out of riders, or methods
for calculating saddle heights, optimal knee position
in relation to pedal spindle and Eastern European
weight-training regimens to be analysed. The notion
of recovery – between races, between stages – never
occupied journalists. The race calendar was packed,
the teams were small and the demands on the body
were heavy.

Maybe we still had Jacques Anquetil's comment
that 'you don't ride the Dauphiné and then
Bordeaux-Paris only on water' at the back of our
minds. The quote, reportedly made on French
TV, was: "*On ne fait pas le Dauphiné et Bordeaux-Paris
en marchant à l'eau claire.*" This was in 1965, when
Anquetil won the Dauphiné Libéré in the Alps, then

travelled west to Bordeaux to start and win that marathon the day after. Such powers of recovery! And maybe we never really asked about the precise nature of a *soigneur*'s job when it came to 'looking after' riders in hotel rooms. It was a leg-rub and application of chamois cream, right?

Our collective blind spot over what, precisely, 'recovery' entailed never seemed like a big issue. Additionally, the idea that some forms of recovery treatment might actually be performance-enhancing doping were quickly overshadowed by 'real' doping stories: tales of blue testosterone pills taken immediately after the stage finish, quaint amphetamines and, latterly, blood doping in all its multifarious forms. Recovery products – the ones invoked by riders who testified at the post-Festina trial – somehow still never seemed like doping. The thinnest of thin excuses that some riders came up with, saying they didn't know they were being doped and assumed the *soigneurs* were injecting them with 'products to help me recover' was no longer an option. We knew that 'doping' was when you took something to make you ride faster for longer. Recovery products were… well, like headache pills, right? That naïve position has now gone – the fig leaf that riders and teams hid behind now blown away.

When Garmin unilaterally introduced its 'no-needles' policy within the team, it was on to something. If carefully monitored and administered doses

of EPO, HGH, packed red blood cells and the rest
were at one end of the medicalisation of cycling,
then those 'recovery' practices, from the widespread use of injections of Ferritin, B12, and iron or
infusions of hydrating saline with added paraceta-
mol or amino acids, were at the other end of that
same pharmacological continuum. So, in 2010, promoted by the team doctor Prentice Steffen, Garmin
said 'stop', and required its riders to sign a contract,
part of which read, 'No injections or infusions of
any kind will be permitted in any racing, training or
resting circumstance, no matter what time of year,
location or event.' Which covers it, and then some.
You would hope that when a rider goes to the dentist
for root canal work, a pain killing injection might be
exempt...

And, 'inspired' by Garmin's lead, at the start of
the 2011 Giro d'Italia in May, the UCI rolled out
a sport-wide 'no-needle' policy, except in specific
medical circumstances. The logic and science were
sound. Having 'needle-happy' medical staff on a
team promoted an unhealthy culture and normalised
the use of injected products of all kinds. And, for Dr
Steffen, there was no sound scientific evidence that
injected or infused 'recovery' products had much
more than a placebo effect anyway. If required, oral
medicines were just as effective.

And, speaking of recovery products and a no-
needle policy, the UCI, supported by the Movement

for Credible Cycling (MPCC) has been trying to clamp down on the indiscriminate use of glucocorticoids. Following on from the no-needle policy, in 2011 the UCI demanded that any rider with a medical reason to receive a cortisone injection should take two days off – effectively removing the possibility of a pre-Classics course of the drug. Turning the screw still tighter, in 2013 the UCI, supported by the MPCC, then insisted that any rider requiring a cortisone treatment had to take eight days out of racing, putting abusers of cortisone out of stage races, too.

With no needles, no infusions of painkillers or any other *soigneur*-special voodoo potions, as well as a clamp-down on cortisone – many riders' favourite not-really-doping product since the 1960s – truly the landscape of modern cycling has changed. Add to that the ADAMS whereabouts programme, increased out-of-competition testing and biological passports, and we've got to a point where if we were still witnessing the same sorts of performances we saw in, say, 1996, we should be worried.

Of course, in some cases, we are seeing similar performances. Or rather, the presumption (please God) is that they're the same but different. Riders are still capable of astonishing physical feats – they are world-class athletes after all – but they aren't capable of sustaining them any more.

'There's a genetic component to winning a Tour, and there's a special psychological make-up you need, too – that desire to work hard – as well as the technical support you have around you, in all the areas that you need,' observed David Millar.

Clearly some bike riders are more professional or just flat-out better than others. Clearly some teams have superior organisation and are more able to prepare their riders for races (coaching programmes, training camps, pre-race stage scouting) than others. But when it comes down to getting into the (literal) shape required to win a Grand Tour, that's not something that you can do on a diet of turnip juice and raw grapefruit, or whatever the current fad diet is. That's a longer-term project, and the sort of thing that takes time. Crash diets and pro-cycling training do not make happy bedfellows – not these days. In February 2004, Lance Armstrong tipped his trainer Michele Ferrari's scales at 79.5kg, which was 5.5kg over where he needed to be by the end of June. A five-and-a-half kilo loss in four months?

Times have changed.

'If guys like Hesjedal and Wiggins are working so incredibly hard – which they are; harder than anyone has ever worked to win these Grand Tours clean… In the old days, you'd do about four months' preparation. You'd turn up fat, take your gear, and off you'd go. Now you have to work for months and months and months, with a massive team of people, living in an oxygen tent, to be able to win clean,' states Millar.

In 1997, in a bar in San Sebastian the night

after Laurent Brochard of France and Festina had won the pro road race world championships, most of the Danish team were topless, sweating, laughing and smashed. They were having a ball – a proper piss-up – and I quit long before they did. Bjarne Riis had silver medallist Bo Hamburger on his shoulders. Christ, I thought – so much for pros living some kind of ascetic lifestyle during the season. Most of them would be lined up again to start the Giro del Piemonte in four days' time. How did they manage that? Ah, right – I get it now – with some help from 'recovery' products.

I dare say riders are still going out on the piss after big results, and who can blame them? It's just that the consequences of such blow-outs might be less easy to recover from. These days, staying on the straight and narrow looks less like an option and more like a contractual obligation, if you want to win clean. Physically, riders are more 'on their own' than they have been for decades. The doping and 'recovery' medicines have been removed from fridges; they're no longer an option.

And then there was Bradley Wiggins's August 2013 decision to 'retreat' from the position of Grand Tour podium contender because it required too much in the way of sacrifices – physical, mental and familial. It's no secret – Wiggins wrote about it in his autobiographies – that after the build-up of pressure that was released after his track triumphs at the

Beijing Olympics in 2008, and then after his win at the 2012 Tour de France and London Olympics, he enjoyed a long period of what might be called 'down time'. The fact that Wiggins also posted a picture on a Twitter account of him and friends 'getting wasted at St Pauls' made it hard to avoid the conclusion that months of living like a hermit can take their toll.

A year later, after a fraught summer of failure at the 2013 Giro d'Italia and his absence from the Tour de France, Wiggins talked about the fact that his Sky team-mate Chris Froome was in a better position to lead the team 'because he didn't have any children'. This, too, is revealing – suggesting that for those riders aiming to win the Tour de France in the modern age, the required training and preparation regimes are incompatible with anything resembling a normal family life.

There's a curious analogy in motorbike racing. The much-repeated saying in the race paddocks of the world is that each child a racer fathers costs him a tenth of a second per lap. But motorbike racers get slower as they get older not because of inescapable physiological decline, but because they lose hunger and appetite. Other than Wiggins, none of the winners of recent Grand Tours – Alberto Contador, Vincenzo Nibali, Froome or Ryder Hesjedal – have children. It's probably a coincidence, but you can bet they all have fairly understanding partners.

It's not just potential Grand Tour winners who

cloister themselves in high altitude retreats, either. Astana's Dane, Jakob Fuglsang, reflecting on his highest-ever Grand Tour result (seventh in the 2013 Tour), realised that his preparation that year had been the best he had ever undergone, and he found himself as captain of a WorldTour team in the biggest race in the sport.

'In the run-up to the Tour I did three altitude training camps in Tenerife, where you ride, eat and sleep, and nothing else. Mentally, it's really tough. Between mid-May and the end of the Tour in July, I was at home in my apartment in Luxembourg for five days. The rest of the time I was at training camps, racing the Dauphiné, and then back in Tenerife to do another training block before the Tour. I can understand why Wiggins says he wants to stop because I don't think people realise the stress and mental effort involved even before you get to the Tour. You have to sacrifice so much all year to be as good as him. Maybe you can do it for a couple of years when you are really hungry for the wins, but when you have achieved your goals, I can understand why you wouldn't be able to keep sacrificing so much.'

Millar's observation, Wiggins's admissions and Fuglsang's realisation are backed up by a rider who finished 38th on general classification of the 2013 Tour de France. Even further down the Tour pecking order than Fuglsang, even when 'only' at the level of Tour stage winner, the stress takes its toll. Christophe Riblon, the Frenchman who saved national honour by winning at the summit of Alpe d'Huez, was shocked at the level of media pressure which fell on him. A brief dalliance in the media glare of the Tour was enough for the Ag2r-La Mondiale rider to appreciate what was required and expected of Wiggins or Froome.

'After the stage win, I never expected so much attention,' said Riblon. 'The media, the questions, the requests and the amount of time it all takes – all the protocols after the stage win – were much, much more than I expected. I can't imagine what it must be like to be in the yellow jersey and to have to do that every day, at that level.'

The answer is that it's clearly stressful, eating into that precious recovery time which can no longer be aided by medication of one kind or another.

Now that pro cycling is this drug-lite environment, where anti-doping measures are more effective and the various 'grey areas', which once aided recovery and training, have been restricted, the dedication required to reach the top is going to change the sport – both as an athletic spectacle as well as putting an end to the long reigns of dominant riders. The notion of an 'era' in cycling is over. The years when Jacques Anquetil, Bernard Hinault, Miguel Indurain or Armstrong dominated the Grand Tours? We won't be seeing those types of reigns again.

Instead, might we be about to see a new generation of younger riders who arrive on the scene, dazzle us for two seasons, and then fade? Are we going to see cycling's equivalent of the 'two-bob rocket' fireworks who end up physically and emotionally burned out by the dieting, the altitude training camps and the absence for months on end from anything like a normal life? For spectators, they would probably say that it's a price worth paying for a dope-free sport, but at what cost to the riders?

Kenny Pryde is a full-time grumpy Glaswegian who has been making a living by arranging words into sentences for money since 1988. Published in the *Guardian, Irish Independent, Herald* and *Scotsman*, he only made it onto the telly once, during the 1998 Tour de France. It's been downhill ever since. In between, he's edited *Winning, mbr* and *SuperBike*.

4

Today, every top cycling team has a bus that combines the need for transport with the luxury of a five-star hotel.

Rupert Guinness remembers the pioneering PDM and ONCE teams, who introduced team buses to the peloton, and charts the rise of the vehicles the riders consider their sanctuary and, almost, their second homes.

ON THE BUSES

BY RUPERT GUINNESS

The team bus. It was an immediate sensation when it arrived on to the cycling scene in 1989, the first being unveiled under the livery of the Dutch PDM team.

The invitation to travel in one was too good to refuse – not just because it would facilitate me interviewing Sean Kelly on the eve of Milan-San Remo, but because it provided the rare experience of enjoying the creature comforts of what was then one of the latest trends in cycling.

I enjoyed the comfort of the plush leather seat while watching the blue ocean pass by as the PDM chauffeur, Rob Van de Merwe, proudly drove the glossy black Mercedes bus from the coastal town San Benedetto, our agreed meeting point on the Adriatic coast. The team had been training there since finishing the Tirreno-Adriatico stage race a few days before, and were heading north to the industrial capital of Milan for the start of 'La Primavera'.

Under the relaxing hum of the engine, I waited for Kelly to summon me to his seat near the front for my audience to chat about the season to come for *Winning Bicycle Racing Illustrated.*

No rush for me. Few outsiders at the time got to travel in a team bus. I was living the dream – or so I thought.

But I was not alone. It was a new experience for Kelly too. The Irishman has just joined PDM from the Spanish Kas team. If anything, in a professional career that by then had spanned 13 years, he was a little wary about travelling all the way to Milan by bus, rather than flying up.

But then, this wasn't the first and only ground-breaking moment for Kelly.

That he had even raced Tirreno-Adriatico was something new: it was the first time that he had pre-pared for Milan-San Remo by taking part in 'The Race of the Two Seas' instead of Paris-Nice, which he had won a record seven times in a row from 1982 to 1988. In those days, even the biggest teams chose between Paris-Nice and Tirreno-Adriatico as their main pre-spring Classics stage race and changes in the race programme were never taken lightly.

'I wasn't too keen about travelling by bus before. But this is different... There's more space,' Kelly told me with a wry smile, as he stretched his legs and lounged back, before adding: 'There's a shower on board, beds to sleep on and cooking equipment.

'There's even a video machine and TV, which is perfect if you are waiting to do a time trial. You can watch the gears the riders use before you, see how they are being affected by the wind and all that.'

Unsurprisingly, it wasn't long before PDM's initiative was copied. The Spanish ONCE team was quick to not only pick up on the team bus idea, but to take the trend one step further by becoming the first team to order and buy two buses, which most of the major teams today have at races around the world.

But it soon wasn't only the black PDM bus or the yellow ONCE bus that would turn heads at race starts. One by one, most of the top teams followed suit, turning what was a novelty into something that was *de rigueur* for any team in the professional peloton that wanted to be taken seriously.

Who will ever forget the va-va-voom of the Dutch TVM team, who travelled the circuit in their Sauna Diana bus, emblazoned with the painting of a naked woman inviting onlookers as she lounged back in true burlesque style?

Sauna Diana was a massage parlour on the Belgian-Dutch border that was owned by one of the TVM riders' parents – and that in itself became an immediate source of attraction to an ever-inquiring media, as their star Australian rider Phil Anderson was reminded during the 1990 Giro d'Italia after he was pipped for the win on the 20th stage between Voghera and La Spezia by Frenchman Laurent Fignon and Italian Maurizio Fondriest.

Within seconds of arriving back at the team

bus, and while still trying to come to terms with his loss, Anderson was asked by an Italian journalist in broken English: 'Phil... Phil... Is it true that Sauna Diana is a house of love?'

Knowing Anderson very well, and his Mount Vesuvius-like reaction to losing big races (the image of his face after Belgian Eddy Planckaert beat him to win the Tour of Flanders in 1988 is forever planted in my memory), it seemed as though time stopped as I waited in anticipation of his answer.

Drawing in breaths as he leaned over his handle-bars in a bid to recover from the sprint finish, Anderson looked up, looked right, sighed and just walked straight into the bus.

I was given the signal to follow and enter with him. Anderson's first words to team staff wondering what had happened outside were, 'Can you believe what that guy asked? If this was a "house of love"!' Then Anderson laughed... much to my relief!

As I sat and listened while interviewing Anderson in the TVM bus about the win that 'could've and should've been, but wasn't', I looked outside and wondered at the teeming mass of fans and media that was circling like swirling krill in the ocean, oblivious to what was really happening, or being said, inside.

Looking back on what was at least a light-hearted incident, witnessing the exchange outside and then observing Anderson's exit strategy to walk off to the bus rather than deal with it there and then – or at least jump into the sweaty, humid and cramped confines of a team car as he would have had to previously – the moment was one that provided my first real experience of the two worlds of a bike race that the team bus has created.

Nevertheless, that has done nothing to diminish the team bus as a draw card. So anticipated is the *grande arrivée* of buses at any major race, it has almost become the curtain raiser for entertainment for cycling fans, while for media and sponsors, it signals the start of business for another day.

All along, as the crowds mill outside the team bus while mechanics prepare bikes, *soigneurs* dash in and out of the bus, and rush back and forth to nearby team cars, attending to various tasks, sports directors attend to media inquiries, and talk with sponsors and fans before the traditional pre-race team meeting inside, the anticipation grows for the first appearance of who everyone is really there to see: the riders.

No question – the team bus is here to stay. Proof of that is found by simply following the snail trail of where buses have come and gone as teams have fallen by the wayside, or even as their customisation to a team's specific needs has led to teams buying new buses and selling off their old ones to other teams. As with bicycles, with every season, the finesse and intricacy of the facilities of the team bus have undergone massive development. They have become a status symbol of perceived strength.

Even before the arrival of their first custom-made bus, the Australian Orica-GreenEdge team management spoke proudly of the bus that would soon be theirs, excited that it would turn heads for being one of the biggest in the bus peloton.

And turn heads it did, as I saw from within by spending a week travelling with the team in one of their two buses – one custom-made in Spain, and the other a second-hand purchase of one of the former Dutch Rabobank team's buses – in the first week of their debut Grand Tour, the 2012 Giro d'Italia.

Perhaps it was just interest in a new team, with its fresh blue, green and white livery but the Orica-GreenEdge bus was always the centre of attention.

However, it was still nothing compared to the attention their bus garnered in the team's second year, in 2013, when, at the 100th edition of the Tour de France, their Basque driver Garikoitz 'Gary' Atxa drove their bus under the finishing arch of stage one from Porto-Vecchio to Bastia, only for it to become stuck – and finally dislodged when the peloton was just five kilometres from the finish.

In the space of a few but seemingly very long minutes, it became the most famous team bus in world sport as a worldwide television audience waited with bated breath to see if Atxa and the race officials could free the bus before the peloton arrived.

Ironically, what was a nightmare day at the office for Atxa turned out to be a publicity dream for Orica-GreenEdge. All publicity is good publicity, they say. Incredibly, too, the main news story of the day was about that bus, rather than the rider who won the stage – Argos-Shimano's Marcel Kittel, whose class was unfairly overlooked, but very quickly corrected in the weeks to come during which the German sprinter took three more stage wins.

After the Tour, the Belgian Omega Pharma-Quick Step team unveiled its newest bus in time for the Eneco Tour stage race in August. According to its press release, the new 13.2-metre-long bus has 'a really powerful 460 engine', and is equipped with nine seats for the riders.

'There is a drawer for all of their belongings, there is electricity, a small table – it's almost like being on a flight,' bus driver Dirk Clarysse proudly explains. 'Just below and behind the seat there is another drawer to store their personal helmet, shoes, and other small cycling equipment.

'We also have two beds so when waiting for a time trial riders can sleep or rest… We have a kitchen, two large showers, and a new satellite system.'

Impressive stuff. So impressive, in fact – and some may argue that this idea came from one too many pichets of rosé – that in 2012 I hatched a plan to organise a bus for the 100th Tour for nine selected media from various countries.

Yes, we joked and laughed about what could have been: the team bus being stocked with fine wines, foie gras and selected cheeses instead of sports drinks, gels, and protein bars. Or perhaps it would be the scene of sweaty hacks showering after another media scrum at the finish line while our laptops were being charged up and placed on our desks in readiness for us to write some sharp and insightful copy for our publications.

To be honest, by 'we' in these talks, I mean anyone in the Tour press corps who was willing to listen to my scheme that peculiarly grew in possibility the more it was spoken about.

I even sourced a bus. Word around the traps was that the old German Milram team bus was available for hire for such ventures. And, dare I admit it, the idea grew to the point of me pitching it verbally during the 2012 Tour to Philippe Sudres, the *chef de presse* at ASO, the Tour organisers, under the guise that it could make a reality television show that would provide a rare behind-the-scenes look at the race.

Sudres even went as far as to nod, smile and say, '*Peut-être... Pourquoi pas?*' [Perhaps... Why not?]

Sudres was suffering from a massive toothache at the time, it has to be said, and might well have given that same reply to any idea that was put before him that day. Probably a good thing, too, as that was where my idea remained – as just an idea.

However, for all the benefits the team bus has provided, has its impact on the sport been for the better? Sure, the advantages are significant for riders, team staff and sponsors whose exposure is heightened as the parking area assigned for them turns into a veritable trade show of their brand and talent.

But, increasingly over the years, many have sensed the team bus has been ruining something that was intrinsically unique to cycling, something that set it apart from other sports: the intimate connection between riders, and the fans and media. The bus gives the riders a shield behind which to hide.

Anecdotes are many and varied about how the team bus works for and against various parties. No one begrudges the principal benefit of them offering riders the optimal environment in which to recover from another tough day in the saddle by washing, eating and rehydrating as soon as possible after a race. The alternative is squeezing into team cars only to then sit in the all-too-frequent traffic jams that are par for the course for anybody trying to get away from a European pro bike race.

But how far has the definition of a 'need' for a team bus been stretched to the detriment of the sport? Almost a quarter of a century since PDM blazed the trail and first parked their team bus at the start of a race, the distance between the riders and the public is as great as it's ever been.

It quickly became clear to the riders that the confines of the black-tinted windows of the team bus provided more than just a place to wash and dress in private, or to hold team meetings. It was also a

place to avoid people. It was a place to strategise
approaches to the media outside who they felt had
wronged them.

To the media, it soon became clear that some
riders would often relish the opportunity to observe
who among the press pack was outside waiting for
an interview, and exact their own form of vengeance
for a report they did not like in several ways.

Riders could get the upper hand by targeting
someone they were at odds with and, with lines of
argument locked and loaded, step out and surprise
them with an impromptu audience. In such a situation, the rider is in full control as the unwary journalist bides his or her time outside, growing increasingly
frustrated by the wait without an inkling for when
the rider they want to speak to might come out – or
if the rider they are about to be confronted with is
even the one they had asked for.

A rider doesn't even need a big bus to execute that
plan either. That, Australia's Stuart O'Grady showed
me in the transitional period of the team bus trend
during the 2004 Tour, when teams were not quite
cashed-up enough to buy plush touring buses, but
invested in luxury camper vans – which are still
in use today, although now more as back-ups for
mountain stages or races with limited access.

The incident was one O'Grady and I were at least
able to laugh about several years later while writing
my book, *What A Ride – An Aussie Pursuit of the Tour*

de France. It all unfolded after stage eight between Lamballe and Quimper, and related to an article I had written for the *Sydney Daily Telegraph* regarding an incident between O'Grady and compatriot Scott Sunderland during the sprint finish the day before from Châteaubriant to Saint-Brieuc in Brittany.

Basically put, O'Grady didn't take too kindly to Sunderland entering the fray of a bunch sprint that offered vital points for the green jersey that he was a contender for, believing Sunderland had no place in it as he was not regarded as a sprinter.

Sunderland, racing in his last Tour, disagreed, and the two riders exchanged words after the stage, and spoke to the media, all of which was reported. Lo and behold, O'Grady didn't take too kindly to my report on it, and let me know it.

As soon as he exited the Cofidis team bus, I saw it in his face – a stony look, with his eyes showing no emotion, instead glaring right at me as the Australian SBS television crew to my right looked on.

'Thanks for the article, mate,' O'Grady said to me. Stalling for time, and knowing what story he was referring to, I replied: 'What article?'

His reply: 'Yesterday's… You made me sound like a ****. And those comments of Scotty.'

O'Grady turned and stepped back into their bus. The door closed. The show was over.

As I looked to the SBS television crew, I noticed their camera was rolling. I made them swear that their footage would end on the cutting-room floor.

I laughed. They laughed. And, to O'Grady's credit, he came out five minutes later and acted as if nothing had happened.

Years ago, I'd told him that if he ever had a beef about something I had written, to let me know, rather than let it fester. He had and I could hardly begrudge him for it. But I never forgot that it showed just how riders could use the confines of their bus to their gain.

Another favourite for the rider is to deliberately wait before exiting the bus until the very last minute, ignoring the journalist – or anyone else they want to avoid – under the guise of not having enough time.

Even upon their return to the bus after a race, riders will say, 'I'll just take a shower first,' knowing full well they won't return, and leaving the team media manager to update you while you're waiting outside, saying the rider you want is still having his shower (no matter how many other riders have arrived since), only for you to eventually realise the ruse is on you when the bus engine starts and the door shuts in your face.

Of course, in the worst-case, and most sinister, scenario, according to *The Secret Race* by Tyler Hamilton, a former team-mate of Lance Armstrong's, and co-author Dan Coyle, the team bus was also a place where some riders would take performance-enhancing drugs ahead of the start of a stage, within metres of fans and media.

Then again, there is little difference between the team bus and a football team's locker room, other than that it is mobile. Why should we be surprised just because it's a bus?

Cycling was different before the team buses first started to appear at race starts. Maybe before they arrived we – media and public – didn't realise how good we had it with the lazy, relaxed starts as riders sat on team-car bonnets, or in seats with the doors open, or even on a nearby curb-side.

Should we push for change? That won't happen. The horse – or team bus – has already bolted. But next time you're at a bike race where riders arrive in cars and not team buses, take a look around and think about it: there was once a time when that was what it was like at the very biggest of races.

They were good days. There were many smiles. And, funnily enough, the *départ* of a race was a relatively stress-free place to be.

But then, professional road cycling has changed in so many ways. Maybe it's best to just remember what was good and make the best of what it is now – which is still a great sport worth following.

Rupert Guinness lived in Belgium and France from 1987 to 1996, but now lives in Sydney, Australia, where he writes for the *Sydney Morning Herald*. He covered his first Tour de France in 1987 and since then has only missed the 1996 and 2007 editions. The 100th Tour in 2013 was his 25th.

5

Amid the calls for ASO to run a women's Tour de France it has perhaps been forgotten that in the 1980s, the Tour Féminin ran alongside the men's race.

Richard Moore speaks to Marianne Martin, the American who won the first Tour Féminin in 1984, just a few weeks before Connie Carpenter-Phinney took the gold medal at the inaugural Olympic women's road race.

NINETEEN EIGHTY-FOUR

BY RICHARD MOORE

*'It was a bright cold day in April,
and the clocks were striking thirteen.'*

It was late June rather than April. And the clocks, contrary to George Orwell's prediction for 1984, in his dystopian novel of the same name, were not striking thirteen. Yet the shock and sense of the unreal – the disruption to the natural order of things – might have been equivalent.

Certainly it was a spectacle that most thought they would never see: 81 years after the first men's Tour de France, a stage race around France for women; perhaps not the seismic change that Orwell forecast for 1984, but pretty significant in its own small way.

A modestly-sized field of 36 women, representing six national teams, set off on June 30th for the first 80-kilometre stage from Bobigny to Saint-Denis. Seven teams had entered, but the Russians withdrew at the last minute. Those who were there were history-makers, competing in the first Tour Féminin, run by the same organisers and using the same roads as the Tour de France. There were 18 stages, none more than 80 kilometres long, all taking place over the final part of the course used, a few hours later, by the men. Félix Lévitan wanted a longer, tougher race, on the same scale as the men's, but Jacques Goddet, Lévitan's co-director of the Tour de France, was against the proposal. Goddet worried about the female riders' ability to urinate on the move.

There was also opposition of the kind articulated in a letter in *La Provence Cycliste*: 'A woman who runs, a woman who jumps, a woman who swims, that's good. A woman who pedals, that's less pretty. Can you see them arriving completely exhausted at Alpe d'Huez or Avoriaz all grey from the dust or black from the mud? Will they dare confront, in this disfigured state, the television cameras without first cleaning up? The feminine ideal could take one hell of a blow.'

Marianne Martin, a 26-year-old from Michigan, but by 1984 resident in the outdoors mecca of Boulder, Colorado, was not thinking of the feminine ideal; she was thinking about winning.

Her introduction to cycle racing had been through the Colorado stage race, the Red Zinger Bicycle Classic, which in 1980 became the Coors Classic. Martin worked in a bar in the hotel that hosted the riders one year; she thinks it was 1977, when there

The United States team – note the team name
is in French, Etats-Unis – at the start of one of
the stages. Marianne Martin is in polka dots.

was a women's race as well as a men's.

Martin had been a ballet dancer, but cycle racing thrilled her – 'It looked exciting, it looked fun' – and when she began racing in 1980, she found she was good at it, especially when the road went up. A year later she read about Jonathan Boyer becoming the first American male to ride the Tour de France, where he stood out in his stars-and-stripes national jersey. (Félix Lévitan was behind Boyer's jersey, too – he wanted to highlight that an American was riding, to help open up the untapped American market.)

'When I read that Jonathan Boyer was doing the Tour,' says Martin, 'I said, "I want to do that one day."'

Within three years, that would become a possibility. It was in January 1984 that Martin learned of the new event. But it wasn't the only historic first that year: the Olympic Games, in Los Angeles, would, for the first time, include a women's road race. The Games began just five days after the Tour, however. It would be difficult, perhaps impossible, to do both.

But this posed no dilemma for Martin. She wasn't interested in the Olympics. She decided she would rather ride the first Tour than win the inaugural women's Olympic road race. First, though, she had to be selected, which wasn't straightforward.

'I was riding badly that year,' she recalls. She was ill, suffering from anaemia. In the end, she was the final rider to be named for the American team. Still, she travelled to France in a mood of excitement and optimism: the Alps would be her stage, where she would stamp her authority and show off her climbing ability. She could hardly wait.

Yet she was going into the unknown. She spoke no French, and nobody there seemed to speak any English. As though to illustrate the point, the clothing she and her team-mates wore was not adorned with 'USA', but the French spelling: 'États-Unis'.

Even more remarkably, the Tour Féminin would be Martin's first race in Europe – and her first outside America.

* * *

The enthusiasm of Martin and her fellow female competitors was not universally reciprocated.

'I like women, but I prefer to see them doing something else,' said Laurent Fignon on the eve of the 1984 Tour, where he would be defending his title. Marc Madiot was a little more progressive. Well, not really.

The French rider – now FDJ team director – said he was in favour of women cycling, but only if they wore more feminine clothing, 'to bring out their qualities better'. Madiot suggested 'white or pink shorts, sleeveless jerseys or gloves and socks with a little lace'.

It will surprise some – because it might not fit with the caricature of the tough, unreconstructed 'Badger' – but Bernard Hinault was a supporter of a women's Tour de France. As black-or-white and matter-of-fact as ever, Hinault said he saw no reason why, if men could race, women could not.

But it was Félix Lévitan, above all, who championed the Tour Féminin. Having directed the Tour with Goddet since 1962, Lévitan wanted the Tour to broaden its horizons, reaching out to America and an even more remote frontier: women. Indeed, the scope of his ambition was admirable; it wasn't just to run a Tour for women, but in doing so to promote gender equality in wider society.

As Lévitan explained: 'For some time now my wife and I have thought that women do not occupy the position they deserve in society. Woman is the equal of man, when she is not superior to him. Biologically that is proven by the medical schools and scientists. Therefore, we thought about organising something greater than anything that had been done to this point in cycling for athletic women.'

Lévitan thought the first women's Tour could be a catalyst; that it would 'give a new dimension to top-flight female cycling'. And it did, briefly. In the mid-1980s, the annual spectacle of Jeannie Longo and Maria Canins sharing the podium with the men's winner in Paris put the leading female riders, if only symbolically, on some kind of equal footing. So did the fact that the winner wore the same yellow jersey. But it didn't last. The Tour Féminin fizzled out, reappearing in different guises, but failing to capture the imagination in the same way that it briefly did three decades ago.

Revived in the early 1990s and renamed the Grande Boucle a few years later, the race sometimes lasted no more than five days. The final edition, held in 2009, was won by Britain's Emma Pooley.

Nineteen eighty-four should have been a pivotal year for women's cycling: year zero. However, the fact that in 2013 the issue of a women's Tour de France was back on the agenda, with a petition organised by some of the leading riders, suggests that it wasn't. It also highlights that cycling remains different to many professional sports in the 21st century.

Women are marginalised, their races second-rate, their presence at the top bike races generally restricted to their roles as podium girls.

It is rarely questioned, other than when something newsworthy happens – such as following the 2013 Tour of Flanders, when Peter Sagan pinched a podium girl's bottom. It is simply the way the way the sport has developed and evolved (or not).

But why? To understand, it is necessary to go back much further than 1984, to the invention of the bike, the origins of the men's Tour de France, and what the machine and the institution came to represent.

* * *

The Tour de France didn't just celebrate masculinity: it promoted 'hypermasculinity', according to the American historian Christopher Thompson. Thompson's book, *Tour de France: A Cultural History*, is fascinating on the gender politics of the Tour, and of the bicycle itself, which, after its invention in the mid-19th century, was enthusiastically taken up by women, to the mounting alarm of men, who saw women cycling 'as representative of a profoundly disturbing development: women's emancipation'.

In France, there was heightened sensitivity to such a phenomenon, claims Thompson, due to a crisis of masculinity, sparked by a plummeting birthrate, the humiliation of the 1870 defeat in the Franco-Prussian war, and the increasing strength of, and threat posed by, neighbouring Germany.

'A variety of social commentators, especially on the Right, were blaming feminism for the decline in France's birthrate,' writes Thompson. 'Any activity that appeared to hinder France's demographic expansion by distracting women from their reproductive duty to the nation became an obvious target... [and] cycling appeared to be just such an activity.' Indeed, 'the trend toward increased female independence came to be personified by women cyclists'.

There were fears that riding a bike could harm a woman's ability to reproduce. Or worse: 'Physi-

cians wondered whether pedalling resulted in female masturbation and might lead women to seek
sexual pleasure on their new machines rather than in
the marital bed.' (To be fair, erroneous fears about
cycling having an adverse effect on reproductive
ability have focused on males, too – though men
have not been accused, at least not by the medical
profession, of using their bikes for sexual pleasure.)

In France, women were openly discouraged from
cycling. They were charged an additional three francs
for cycling lessons, and racing came to be frowned
upon, though women had raced almost from the
machine's inception, in a series of women-only
events in Bordeaux in 1868, and then with the men
in Paris-Rouen a year later. In Paris-Rouen, five
women started in the 100-rider field, and one placed
29th. But in 1891, seven women entered the 1200km
Paris-Brest-Paris, only for the organisers to tell them,
'Non' – which put them in line with Baron de Cou-
bertin, the founder of the modern Olympic Games,
who was generally opposed to women's sport.

'The underlying assumption appears to have been
that France possessed a finite amount of virility,'
writes Thompson. 'If women were becoming more
masculine, men must therefore be undergoing a
process of feminization, becoming what Maurice
Barres contemptuously dismissed as "demi-males".'
(Female fashions such as culottes were also partly
inspired by cycling – they were easier to ride in than

skirts. But they were also seen as less feminine.)

On October 17th, 1912 the Union Vélocipedique de France declared that races for women would no longer be sanctioned. By then, the Tour de France was nine years old, and already well established as the ultimate test of strength, endurance and suffering – or masculinity. It also served as a metaphor for war (as our old friend George Orwell also pointed out with regard to sport).

The men went off to 'do battle' with each other while the women stayed at home, a point empha-sised by the Tour's founding newspaper, *L'Auto*, whose prose painted florid pictures of the pretty female fans by the roadside, and the women – mothers and wives – left at home.

Before one early Tour, the paper described one woman's 'moist look, heavy with tenderness and inexpressible love' for her husband: 'A handsome fellow who leaves for the Tour a little as for war.' They published anecdotes about how the wives and girlfriends coped: 'They certainly experience emotions, the little wives of our racers... with their glorious husbands.'

All of this helped reinforce traditional gender roles: the men were rugged, strong and independent; the women were pretty, passive, and provided emotional support.

These roles would prove remarkably enduring, and to some extent persist to this day. The TV audience in France has always been said to comprise a high proportion of women – or housewives – with advertising targeted accordingly. And the tradition of riders receiving fan letters – frequently a euphemism for love letters – only died with the advent of the internet, with Richard Virenque perhaps the last 'housewives' favourite'. Before him, Charly Gaul reportedly received up to 60 letters a day, many of them, so the legend goes, from married women.

Another tradition that helps sustain the idea that the riders are like soldiers going off to war are those occasions when a ceasefire is called, with the rider given leave by the peloton to ride ahead and greet his family. And the annual reunion in Paris, where the wives and girlfriends arrive to meet the returning heroes, still has something of the atmosphere of a wartime homecoming.

During the race itself, women (other than podium girls) make only fleeting appearances – usually on rest days. It isn't quite as bad as in 1939, when Victor Cosson was fined 50 francs for the repeated presence on the route of his fiancée in a support vehicle. But Greg LeMond's wife, Kathy, was a trailblazer in the 1980s when she extended her stay beyond rest days, even sharing a room with Greg on occasions. More recently, Michelle Cound, the fiancée of 2013 Tour champion Chris Froome, complained that when she attended her first race, the 2012 Critérium International, she was told to eat at a different table to Froome and his team-mates.

'It was a little bit strange, even walking into the dinner hall,' says Cound. 'There were other teams, and the riders would all look. You could see them thinking, "Why is there a woman here?"' ('Segregation is *de rigueur* for the warrior's rest,' said Jacques Anquetil's wife, Janine, in the 1960s.)

A limited female infiltration of the Tour began in the press room. In the 1940s, *L'Humanité*, the Communist newspaper, sent Hélène Parmelin – a novelist as well as a journalist – to the race, where Italian cycling legend Gino Bartali asked her, since she was swanning around France, who was taking care of domestic duties. She replied that her husband was looking after the home. Twenty years later, another female journalist, Huguette Debaisieux, covered the Tour for *Le Figaro*. Her conclusion: 'The Tour is, with the stock exchange, the National Assembly and the Council of State, one of the last bastions that women have not really succeeded in infiltrating.'

Certainly one or two female voices in the press room were, and are, all but insignificant when set against a prevailing culture perhaps best exemplified by the continued presence of podium girls. Could there be a more potent symbol of male power and female subservience? Because, arguably, the women are not there to look beautiful; rather, their primary function is to make the riders appear desirable. And given that most are emaciated-looking men in lycra, with shaved legs, they need all the help they can get. One of the ironies and paradoxes of the Tour as the ultimate test of masculinity is that so many of its champions are so far from the masculine ideal in terms of their build.

When podium girls were introduced is not entirely clear, but in 1947 there was a Miss Tour de France competition, and, in the years before that, there were local beauty contests along the route, with the winner invited to meet the winner of the stage. And so really it was the men, not the women, who were supposed to be the objects of desire.

'They push each other, they bump each other, they press forward,' said an early report in *L'Auto* of the female fans, '[and] given the chance, they would like to feel the steel muscles to make sure that a little motor is not hidden in them.'

It was way back in 1909 when a women's Tour de France seems to have been first proposed, by a female reader who made the suggestion in a letter published in *L'Auto*. The paper responded that it was impossible, since it would require 'razing the mountains' (which clearly women would be incapable of climbing – yet, interestingly, this was a year before the Pyrenees were included in the men's race). A decade or so later, another sports paper, *Sportives*, commented: 'That sportswomen go on rides for fun, nobody can object to that, but that women speed "like giants of the road", no, one hundred times no!'

It wasn't until the 1950s that women's racing was officially recognised. The Fédération Française de Cyclisme (FFC) and UCI created female road racing championships; the UCI also recognised female records. And in 1955 a Tour Féminin Cycliste was organised, held over five days, and 372km, with 48 starters and 37 finishers. But it was not held again.

Very slowly, the number of females taking out racing licences with the FFC increased, from 34 in 1960, to 400 in 1975, to 1,500 in 1982. It was a modest proportion of the total membership (no more than three per cent), but hardly an insignificant number. Perhaps thanks to that, and to Lévitan, and to other pressures that were beginning to tell in the wider world of sport, in particular with the Olympic Games, a women's Tour de France was finally on the agenda.

* * *

And yet, was it a coincidence that the first women's Tour came along in 1984, which really was year zero for women's sport more broadly?

The women's road race at the Olympics in Los Angeles was not just the first road race: it was the first time any women's cycling events had been included in the Games, although the women had to make do with just a road race; the track was still deemed out-of-bounds. But the road race, won by

Connie Carpenter-Phinney (current pro Taylor Phinney's mother), received scant attention. The focus was all on another race, for many the ultimate endurance event: the marathon, with the 1984 Games representing the end to a long, arduous campaign. A marathon in itself, you could say.

It was the marathon that provided the most potent symbol, that crystalised the debate about women's sport, which revolved around one question: were women up to it? Prior to 1984, the longest track event for women was the 1,500 metres, and that was only introduced in 1972. Even the 800 metres was absent between 1928 and 1960, after several female competitors collapsed, exhausted, at the Paris Games in 1924.

The pioneer was Kathrine Switzer, who entered the Boston Marathon in 1967, using only her initials. When the officials realised she was female, they tried to accost her during the race, but she was defended by male club-mates, who formed a protective cocoon. The pictures of the confrontation caused a minor scandal, and empowered Switzer to take up the fight. She campaigned and helped organise women-only events and, finally, the first women's marathon sanctioned by the world governing body, the IAAF, was held in Tokyo in 1979. It was attended by Adriaan Paulen, the IAAF president, who subsequently announced that he would support the addition of women's races of 5,000 metres, 10,000 metres and the marathon to the Olympic programme.

And so it came to pass that in 1984 the first women's marathon was held. For those opposed to it, mainly on the grounds that women were incapable of running such a distance, and that it was bad, even dangerous, for their health (a century after similar fears were expressed for female cyclists, reproductive ability was cited as one of the big risks), their fears appeared to be confirmed when a Swiss runner, Gabriela Andersen-Scheiss, entered the Coliseum and was barely able to run. She appeared drunk as she staggered around the track, rejecting the approaches of medical officers (it's on YouTube, of course, and makes for a gruesomely compelling spectacle). It took her six minutes to do one 400-metre lap. She finished 37th in a time of 2.48.45 (the winner, Joan Benoit, was 14 minutes quicker), then collapsed. But she was okay.

That the first Olympic women's road race, over 50 miles (79.2km), attracted only a fraction of the attention was perhaps symptomatic mainly of cycling's lower profile, compared to that of athletics. Carpenter-Phinney's winning time was also a bit quicker than Benoit's: two hours, 11 minutes. But it was equally historic, especially for the hosts, with Carpenter-Phinney having become the first American cyclist to win an Olympic medal since 1912. Rebecca Twigg, her fellow American, won silver and thus became the second. Forty-four women finished the road race: a

South Korean, Son Yak-Seon, was last, 37 minutes, 22 seconds behind Carpenter-Phinney.

Connie Carpenter, as she was then known, had competed in the 1972 Winter Olympics, aged just 14, but turned to cycling after suffering an ankle injury. She then won the Red Zinger Bicycle Classic in 1977 – the same event that had so enthused Marianne Martin, then working as a barmaid in a Colorado hotel. But two years after that, Carpenter quit, fed up with the lack of races for women. She returned for the 1984 Olympics, then retired for good. At 27, Los Angeles was her last race.

* * *

Five days before Carpenter-Phinney's gold medal ride, history was made in Paris when the first Tour Féminin finished. The pre-race favourite was an American, Betsy King, who had been racing in France all season, and who had entered Bordeaux-Paris, the now-defunct longest classic on the calendar, at 560km.

For taking on the men in such a gruelling event, King received a lot of publicity. Even the *New York Times* took an interest.

'I'm doing this to say, "Hey, man, we count, too. Women are important,"' said King. Yet she admitted that she was dreading it: 'I look forward to this as much as you look forward to getting your wisdom teeth out. But it has to be done. A lot of people think women can't ride a race like this. So somebody's got to do it to show them a woman won't die.' In the event, King finished only ten minutes behind the winner, Hubert Linard.

But King was nowhere when the Tour Féminin got under way. The opening stages were dominated by a powerful Dutch team. Mieke Havik won the first two stages; on the first, a British rider, Helen Parritt, fell and broke her collarbone. She was the only rider not to finish, which testifies either to the toughness of the assembled field, or the fact that – as Lévitan feared – it wasn't enough of a test.

The Dutch domination continued: Petra de Bruin won stage three to Béthune; Helene Hage won stage four to Cergy-Pontoise, where the Dutch filled the top five places; Havik won her third stage the next day, to Alençon; Connie Meyer continued the run on stage six, to Nantes. And the next day, to Bordeaux? De Bruin again. Seven stages, seven Dutch wins.

'The mountains will sort the Dutch out – even they think so,' said Alec Taylor, the British team manager. 'So they make hay while the sun shines.'

Finally, on stage eight to Pau, there was a first non-Dutch victory thanks to Kelly-Ann Way of Canada. But, now in the south of France, and heading east towards the Alps, there was disquiet at the length of the transfers. The logistics of holding a women's Tour on the same roads as the men's race, usually on the final 80km of the stage, before the publicity caravan came through, meant that the riders had to be driven long distances. After the stage to Bordeaux, the transfer was 300km. Some were not happy, but Marianne Martin was sanguine.

'I didn't think the transfers were a big deal at all,' she says. 'We got to see all of France. We just got in the car and they took us.'

For Martin the whole experience was an adventure. After being the last rider called up to the American team, she travelled, at her own expense, from her home in Boulder to New York. From there, the team – or the Tour organisers, who covered all costs – took care of the expenses.

'I was working as well,' says Martin. 'There weren't professional women riders; we weren't allowed to make money from the sport. So I did jobs, anything I could. And I paid for myself to get to New York. And you know what? That was fine by me.'

Martin was third on stage one, but she was biding her time, waiting for the Alps. Already she could see that King, the notional team leader, was not up to it. Bordeaux-Paris had not killed her, but near enough.

'I think that did her in,' says Martin. 'I don't think she recovered from that.

'When climbing's your strength, you see who's strong and who's not,' Martin continues. 'You watch people, but the climbing separates everyone.'

But before the battleground of the Alps, the

Dutch domination continued: De Bruin won stage nine, and another Dutchwoman, Henneke Lieverse, won stage ten, before Havik claimed her fourth to Rodez.

On stage 12, Martin struck. It was a hilly 62km from La Chapelle-en-Vercors to Grenoble, and she attacked early on the Côte de Chalimont – a first-category climb. The only rider with her was Judith Painter, a British rider recovering from crash wounds, including an infected arm. Martin remembers 'a British girl... We were riding together, and at one point she started to pass me and I thought, "No, you can't do that…"'

Martin left Painter and won the stage alone, claiming a minute-and-a-half on Hage, who was still in yellow. Now Martin was second, just over a minute down. She was enjoying the climbs, though she told reporters in Grenoble: 'They were not as tough as I expected, but there was certainly a lot more switch-back to them.' Back home in Colorado, she was used to climbs that went straight up.

The next day – stage 13 – was a 20km mountain time trial. Hage won, with Martin third at 38 seconds. Next, a summit finish at La Plagne. And while, in the men's race, Fignon all but put the seal on his second successive title with his third stage win at the Alpine ski resort, Martin did the same in the women's race.

'The Dutch team that day were attacking and counter-attacking,' she says. 'It was the hardest day

Martin wins her stage of the Tour Féminin at
Grenoble in the Alps. The climbs were not as
tough as she was used to in Colorado, she said.

of the race.' But by the end of the stage she had the yellow jersey, and she led Hage, who won the next day to Morzine, by a commanding 3-17.

Martin says that her contact with the men was limited: 'One night, I don't remember where, they took a couple of us over to the hotel where the men's teams were. It was me and the Dutch girl in yellow [Hage], and there was Fignon, [Vincent] Barteau and all the rest of them. And they pointed to Fignon and said, "He's gonna win." And I remember thinking to myself, "I'm gonna win."

'A lot of the time,' Martin continues, 'I didn't know what was going on, because I didn't speak French. But it was great; it was a fabulous time. It was so authentic.'

After stage finishes she would get changed, 'grab a bunch of American hats', and go out into the crowd, waiting for the men's race, swapping hats for souvenirs. One conversation sticks in her mind: 'I was in the restricted area talking to somebody from one of the news stations. He asked me what I was doing there, I told him, and he said: "I didn't know there was a women's Tour." And this was the last day!'

The fans by the roadside, she says, were encouraging and, as far as she could tell, entirely supportive.

'I thought it was fabulous in every single sense. We were well taken care of. The people were fabulous: the people who worked on the Tour, the people in the towns, the fans.'

Two Americans in Paris. Martin on the podium with Tour winner Fignon and Greg LeMond.

Martin had an interest in photography – these days she works as a portrait photographer in Boulder – and chatted to the photographers. Or tried to chat.

'I didn't speak to them very well, but we communicated, and they all sent me photos afterwards. So I have a great photo album from the Tour.'

The pictures show Martin, in her États-Unis kit, small, compact, with shoulder-length strawberry-blonde hair, frequently smiling, often in the polka-dot mountains jersey which she also won, usually out of the saddle, attacking the climbs on which she excelled. Then finishing alone at La Plagne, and gulping down a bottle of Perrier. Like Sean Kelly, she rode a Vitus aluminium bike, and she still has her Tour-winning machine, hanging up in her garage. And she has one yellow jersey, having given the others away.

'It's in my closet,' she says. 'I don't really have any pictures up. You could come into my house and never know about that part of me.'

And then there are the pictures in Paris, of the women's field on the Champs-Elysées, and of Martin on the podium with – and alongside – such familiar faces: Fignon, second-placed Bernard Hinault, third-placed Greg LeMond. In one picture she and Fignon stand holding hands in the air. In another, LeMond – hailed as the first American ever to make the podium of the Tour, even as he is standing beside an American in yellow – is caught sneaking a glance at Martin, a bemused expression on his face. Martin says it was their first meeting 'on the podium together, but I didn't chit-chat with him'. She didn't realise that Lévitan was the man to thank. 'He congratulated me, gave me his card, but I didn't know he was behind the women's Tour. If I had, I'd have been all over him.'

And then there are the pictures from later that night in Paris. Martin holding a small American flag, sticking her tongue out, pulling a face for the camera. Looking out from the balcony of the Hôtel de Ville at the enormous crowds. And in a nightclub, sitting with Fignon and Cyrille Guimard, Fignon's *directeur sportif*, who is sporting a bizarre combo of white jacket, no shirt and black bow-tie. And Martin and Fignon each raising a glass of champagne, toasting their success. And finally Martin drinking straight

At the post-Tour party with Laurent Fignon and a bare-chested, tuxedoed Cyrille Guimard.

from an enormous champagne bottle, which almost dwarfs her, while Fignon looks the other way.

Martin went home with $1,000 in prize money. Her life did not change. The local newspaper in Boulder published 'a teeny tiny story'. But other people sent her magazine articles, 'with a full page or something. And a couple of towns flew me out to do presentations and be part of an event'.

The women's Tour was overshadowed by the Olympics, but Martin didn't mind: 'It didn't even matter to me. Connie was from my home town, and she got loads of press, and deservedly so. But I didn't care. I would rather have done the Tour. I would rather win the Tour than the Olympics. I know the Olympics are historic, but to me the Tour de France was the ultimate. It was such a test of your body.

You'd wake up in the morning and think, "There's no way I can ride my bike, I can't even walk downstairs." Yet every day you get on your bike and your body just does what it needs to do.

'Winning was lost on me, in a way,' she continues, 'because I'm a behind-the-scenes person. Riding into Paris in yellow felt half unreal and half amazing. The crowds were un-*believ*-able. But I can't say I dwelt on the history of it all. Just riding it was amazing. Forget winning. Being part of it was just amazing.

'And I felt really strong. I felt I really deserved it.'

* * *

In France, the reaction to the event was mainly positive, albeit couched in the sexist language of the day. *L'Equipe* expressed its disapproval of 'the misogynous world of cycling', and in the next breath asserted that the female cyclists 'had no reason to envy any other female athlete with regard to beauty and charm'.

They had legs like models, said some commentators. And 'in the mountains they are even more beautiful', noted *Libération*. The women cyclists were, according to *Le Figaro*, 'astonishing Amazons... One is forced to note that cycling does not take away the beauty of these graceful persons, who take great care of their appearance.... [and] demonstrated their beauty, proving that top-flight competition and femininity were not incompatible'.

But there was genuine admiration, too. 'One must acknowledge that all these representatives of the so-called weak sex demonstrated exceptional physical and moral capacities to finish the Tour,' was *Le Figaro*'s ultimate verdict. And for *Le Monde*: 'We have learned that they know how to suffer, a cardinal virtue in such an event.'

Martin, who suffered ill health again in 1985 and never returned to the Tour Féminin, is sad that the event did not, as Félix Lévitan hoped, become to women's cycling what the original Tour is to men's. She feels an opportunity was lost.

'You can't just say, "Women's sport is equal to men's," and have women's racing be as exciting as men's and have the same heroes,' she says. 'You can't just make it the same. It takes time. In the 1980s it was establishing itself. But it needed time, and it wasn't given time.'

Richard Moore is a freelance journalist and author. His first book, *In Search of Robert Millar*, won Best Biography at the 2008 British Sports Book Awards, and he is also the author of *Slaying the Badger* and *Sky's the Limit*. He is a former racing cyclist who represented Scotland at the 1998 Commonwealth Games and Great Britain at the 1998 Tour de Langkawi, but didn't cover himself in glory at either. His most recent book is *Tour de France 100*, a photographic history of the first 100 editions. With distinguished colleagues such as Lionel Birnie and Daniel Friebe, he also co-hosts the Humans Invent cycling podcast.

6

Ever since Phil Anderson placed
Australia on the cycling map in
the early 1980s, the nation has
become a dominant force.

Part of the reason was the
creation of a cycling programme
at the Australian Institute of
Sport in 1991.

But what happens to the latent
talents who initially slip the net?
Do they simply miss out?

Anthony Tan discovers that,
fortunately, the answer is no.

THE ONES WHO (ALMOST) GOT AWAY

BY ANTHONY TAN

If I asked you what Jonathan Cantwell, William Clarke, Mitchell Docker, Simon Gerrans, Nathan Earle, Nathan Haas, Adam Hansen, Heinrich Haussler, Mathew Hayman, Lachlan Morton, Richie Porte, Rory Sutherland, Steele Von Hoff and Cameron Wurf all have in common, the first thing you'd probably tell me was that they're all Australian. A likely second might be that they're all riding for, or have ridden for, WorldTour teams.

What else?

Well, none of them are a product of the Australian Institute of Sport (AIS) – the world-class athletic facility that was set up in the national capital of Canberra in 1981. (Some may have spent a bit of time there as part of the national team, when it comes to events like the Olympic Games or world championships, but none of the aforementioned would be considered graduates of the AIS cycling programme.)

Although the idea of a national institute of sport was first mooted in 1973 – based on studies of sports institutes in Europe and their success in developing elite athletes – and considered a feasible option in 1974 by the federal government, the real catalyst came after the country's lamentable showing at the 1976 Olympics in Montreal, where, after eight gold medals at the previous Games in Munich, not one gold was earned by the contingent from Down Under. And so, on Australia Day – January 26th – 1981, the AIS was officially opened by Prime Minister Malcolm Fraser, with renowned swim coach Don Talbot as its inaugural director.

The mission statement was clear: 'Develop elite sport in Australia by providing facilities and funding to sporting organisations and potential elite athletes.' Translation: Find and develop individuals who can win Olympic gold medals. The eight original sports were basketball, gymnastics, netball, soccer, swimming, tennis, track and field, and weightlifting. Of the 800 athletes who applied, 152 scholarships were awarded. A track cycling programme, based in Adelaide, South Australia (home to the Tour Down Under – the first event on the WorldTour calendar), was established in 1987, with the sport also included as one of eight activities in Canberra's Intensive Training Centre facility in 1989.

Two years later, in 1991, having courted the services of East German coach Heiko Salzwedel, the AIS established a men's road cycling and mountain biking programme was established in Canberra.

Before too long, the AIS produced a world-class coterie of graduates including Robbie McEwen, Cadel Evans, Patrick Jonker, Henk Vogels, Matt White, Nick Gates and Kathy Watt – the latter winning the women's road race at the 1992 Olympic Games in Barcelona, as well as a silver medal in the individual pursuit on the track, firmly placing Aussie women on the professional cycling map.

Today, and now operating within the Australian Sports Commission (ASC), responsible for encouraging and developing general participation as well as high performance sport, around 700 scholarships are offered across 36 programmes in 26 different sports, with roughly 75 full-time coaches. A large chunk of the other 200-odd AIS staff are employed in the area of sports science and medicine, which includes sports nutrition, performance analysis, skill acquisition, physiology, recovery, biomechanics, athlete career education, strength and conditioning, psychology, sports medicine, physical therapies, talent identification and applied performance research.

Headquartered on a 65-hectare site in the Canberra suburb of Bruce, AIS programmes are also based around the country – in Sydney, Melbourne, Brisbane, the Gold Coast, Adelaide and Perth – and, for certain sports, including cycling, there are overseas bases in Spain, Italy and the United Kingdom. On March 3rd, 2011, the ASC opened the AIS European Training Centre in Varese, Italy, about 50 kilometres north-west of the business and fashion capital of Milan, originally catering for cyclists and rowers but now extending to golf, boxing, walking, sailing, basketball and wheelchair basketball. It also doubles as the European base for Australia's first WorldTour team, Orica-GreenEdge, which made its debut in 2012.

Today, the modus operandi of the AIS remains unchanged – even if the wording of their mission statement has: 'To provide young Australians with the opportunity to develop their ultimate sporting potential.'

While individuals can apply each July for a coveted scholarship, advertised in the national press, the more common path nowadays is by talent identification via local, state or national sporting organisations, or events organised by said groups.

More recently, AIS scouts have visited schools around Australia, where they ask participants to undergo a series of basic exercises and attempt to match an individual's natural talent with a particular sport, which, more than likely, they haven't thought about trying.

Should they excel, they are then taken through an Intensive Training Centre program, since we all know talent only gets you so far; it is experience, coaching and guidance that harnesses and cultivates that aptitude into what may one day be an exceptional athlete, capable of winning Olympic gold medals, or, in the case of Cadel Evans in 2011, the Tour de France.

But what happens to those who aren't spotted at school, or at their local club meet, or at state or national level competitions? What happens to the unseen or latent talents? The square pegs that don't fit the round holes?

Five of those previously mentioned Australian pros – including Richie Porte, Chris Froome's right-hand man at the Tour de France, who is set to lead Team Sky at the 2013 Giro d'Italia – owe their careers in part to a man who is largely forgotten. As forgotten, in fact, as the part of this wide, brown land he hails from. Unless you are from here, you are unlikely to have heard of him but the fact is, those riders might have slipped the net if it wasn't for him.

* * *

A first-generation Australian from Launceston in Tasmania – the second-largest city, after capital Hobart, on the apple-shaped isle that is the butt of many jokes for those on the mainland (inbreeding being the most common jape) – Andrew Christie-Johnston comes from Scottish and English parentage. Standing about five foot eight, stocky, if not slightly rotund, red-haired – often referred to as a 'ranga', short for orangutan in Aussie slang – and barrel-chested, the 42-year-old looks nothing like a road cyclist or a former one; a track sprinter, maybe.

He used to be a bit of a 'Sport Billy', though: a
state representative in soccer and swimming – the
latter Australia's highest-profile Olympic sport – and
good enough to be state champion in the 200-metre
butterfly in his early teens.

'But I didn't do any more than rank in the top
ten in Australia,' he demurs. 'I'd say in sport terms, I
was pretty good at most sports, but not really good
at any of them. Around the same time, I had a next-
door neighbour – this guy, Ian Leighton – and Ian
used to ride a bit of the Six-Day circuit. And yeah, I
bought a bike and went pedalling with Ian, and started doing some racing. I later dropped the swimming,
then dropped the soccer, and just fell in love with
the sport.'

Racing both the track and road – like most young-
sters did back then in Tasmania, and still do – by his
late teens, as much as he loved it, Christie-Johnston
probably knew he wasn't going to be able to make
cycling his vocation. And so, aged 19, and in the middle of a civil engineering degree at the University of
Tasmania's Launceston campus, where he was also
working part-time as a sheet-metal worker, when an
offer came to work for a firm in Sydney, he decided
to leave his studies and sport behind.

'I went up there and sport just got dropped for,
like, three years. I was working in an engineering firm
and it was all about work. That was the end of any
sporting aspirations I had, back in 1990.

'From that point onwards, I was away from every-one that I knew in Tassie. When I came back, having been transferred with my business, I got back into cycling. I just jumped back on board with my bike, with my cycling buddies, but it was already too late for me to have any aspirations about going anywhere, because I decided I was going down the career path as an engineer. I was only 26 and still felt like I could beat everyone… but I couldn't.'

Bill Johnson, the owner of the sheet-metal factory he worked at in Launceston, and who he got to know well, turned out to be a wealthy Tasmanian businessman with a number of ventures to his name. One of Johnson's fledgling enterprises was Praties (pronounced pray-tees) – a mostly takeaway restau-rant, so-named after a type of Irish potato. (Unsur-prisingly, the menu's staple consists of a giant baked spud or 'jacket potato' – 450 grams, to be precise, for their 'meal-time' option – with a range of 20 to 30 toppings, hot or cold, plonked on top, taking the dish to a near kilo-sized load, selling for ten to 12 Aussie dollars. Curried spuds are their biggest seller, in case your stomach's grumbling.)

After a few years, with five outlets established across the state, Christie-Johnston was asked if he was interested in getting on board, literally.

'He gave me a call and said: "Would you be keen on joining the board?" I had been working for a few firms already in my career, and I just thought it'd be good to get into something myself. I already worked in one of his firms while I was at uni, and I just thought there was an opportunity there, so I took the risk, more than anything. He offered me shares in the company, and, as time went on, I basically bought out all the other shareholders, and then owned the company outright.'

In 1998, Christie-Johnston incurred an injury that kept him off the bike for three months; he began coaching one of his mates – a guy named Steve Price – who he would become business partners with at Praties.

'We talked about setting up a team. I started looking after Steve and different members of the team, which was really a bunch of mates – we weren't real good – and started going to different races.'

Two years later, at the start of the National Road Series (NRS) – Australia's top-level domestic cycling calendar – and with no fanfare, the pair began their journey, funded by their one and only naming rights sponsor, Praties. That is, themselves.

'We decided to do a bit of marketing for the business, but it was more of a passion. I just tried to help out some talented Tasmanian riders. I think when we first started, we had about $10,000. We only had about four guys that we sent away [to races]… Four or five – I'm getting too old to remember. All we did, really, with that $10,000 was put it towards certain costs. But guys still had to pay their airfares, things like that. It was more like sharing costs, with a little bit of extra cash. And that was to get a couple of things like jerseys, pay for a bit of the accommodation, and pay for car hire and stuff, so…'

He wasn't paying the riders, then?

He laughs. 'No.'

* * *

With an annual turnover of roughly four to five million dollars, depending on the year, the eponymous cycling team was limited in what they could do. Ownership of the Praties restaurant chain was now split between Christie-Johnston, his sister and Price, in a roughly 40-30-30 split.

'Our business, it's accessible in terms of providing us with a nice income, but not profitable enough to afford any big investment into cycling. We need to find outside, commercial partners,' says Christie-Johnston, highlighting the fundamental quandary all teams, domestic through to WorldTour, face each year in order to survive.

'It's only a very small business – we only have five outlets in Tasmania. And we don't really have any plans, at this stage, to go any further outside of Tasmania. It's just one of those things that gives Steve and me enough income to do what we love, and that's spend time in cycling.'

For the first ten years, the cash to fund and

operate the team came entirely from their own back pockets. However, in 2010, after Praties rider William Clarke topped the individual NRS rankings the previous season, Genesys Wealth Advisers, a financial planning group then owned by insurance giant AXA Asia Pacific (which later merged with AMP, another Australasian financial services provider, in March 2011), took up title sponsorship of the team, enabling some of their riders to be paid a wage.

'When Genesys Wealth Advisers came on board, that gave us the ability to take a more semi-professional approach to it,' says Christie-Johnston. 'We had enough to run the team when I was looking after it, but not enough to pay the wages.'

By season's end, and after six races, out of the 14 participating teams, the Genesys cycling outfit had become the top-ranked team in the NRS. And, for every year since, they have continued to be.

In 2013, world-renowned Tasmanian fish supplier Huon Salmon adopted a co-naming rights sponsorship with Genesys, upping the team's cash budget to approximately $300,000, and allowing five of their 16 rostered riders – Jo Cooper, Jai Crawford, Nathan Earle, Anthony Giacoppo and Patrick Shaw – to be paid a calendar-year base salary of between $10,000 and $30,000.

'They're not going to get wealthy out of it, but we have a bonus system from our sponsors that is quite significant. If a rider gets a base salary of $30,000,

I'd say he would make another $20,000 to $30,000 in bonuses and prize money in a year, meaning that our top riders would be on $50,000 to $60,000 a year. Even the non-paid riders get benefits out of bonuses. And they come from our sponsors. They reward success, basically.'

Topically, in the wake of Lance Armstrong's confession to Oprah, and, closer to home, the drugs scandal to hit Australian sport that affected Australian rules football and rugby league, the nation's two most popular football codes, Huon's marketing agency created a national advertising campaign that suggested that if you're going to enhance your performance, you should do it naturally, linking the health benefits of their salmon product with increased performance, with the commercials running during the Tour de France.

At the time of writing, at the end of August 2013, and with seven of the 14 NRS events completed, the team had six riders – including the first two, in Nathan Earle and Jack Haig – in the top ten places on the individual rankings, and were on target to claim the best team title on aggregate. As the best-ranked squad on the UCI Oceania Tour, they had also qualified for a spot in the team time trial at the world road championships in Florence, although the costs of travelling for an event they were unlikely to medal in – it would be unrealistic to think they could beat the top WorldTour teams – would likely make such a journey both prohibitive and unproductive.

Huon Salmon-Genesys don't get to do as many races in Asia as they would like, but at the UCI 2.1-ranked Tour of Japan in May, New South Welshman Ben Dyball (the team now recruits riders from the mainland) won the coveted mountain time trial stage to Mount Fuji, before Earle, destined to join his friend and fellow Tasmanian Richie Porte at Team Sky in 2014, won a difficult circuit race the next day.

About mooted plans to take his team from a UCI Continental-registered team to the Pro Continental level, Christie-Johnston says: 'Through the years, we've always tried to find commercial partners, and then with whatever shortfall in the team, we've picked it up off our own sponsorship, to make sure we meet our own budget. To take that next step to Pro Conti, it can't come from us… Basically, we're not wealthy enough.'

Along with Huon Salmon, a new, yet-to-be-named title sponsor was confirmed to join for the 2014 season, but it wasn't going to be enough to 'do it properly', Christie-Johnston told me back in June.

'We've looked at it, and I think we could do it for $1.6 million. I think that's about the minimum. But I'd prefer closer to $2 million, because we've always prided ourselves on whatever we commit to, we do it properly. So I don't like to have the minimum budget. At the end of the day, we will have a bigger budget next year – a far bigger budget than we do this year – but it won't be big enough to go Pro Conti in 2014. We're now talking to people about 2015.'

Most likely referencing the Pegasus debacle of 2010, which left close to 20 riders, including Robbie McEwen, Rohan Dennis and Christian Knees, scrambling for an 11th-hour contract when the 2011 season had already started, Christie-Johnston says 15 years of running his own company has taught him that prudence takes precedence over PR.

'At the end of the day, in cycling – especially on the management side of it – you need to know how to deal with people, to make good business decisions. This is the business sense in me, in that I don't like rushing anything... Pro Conti is something we'd like to be, but it's not that important to us, with everything that comes with it: I'd need to take risks about putting the paperwork in, pay the deposit [bank guarantee] – to perhaps then find out that the money isn't there. I'm not going to make the same mistakes that some other teams have. I'm doing it the other way: I'm making sure I've got the money well in advance. But we're definitely trying to proceed for Pro Conti status for 2015.'

With a change of ownership as a result of AXA being bought out by AMP, Christie-Johnston and Price were unsure whether Genesys Wealth Advisers, their partner of four years, would be continuing their involvement in 2014, other than knowing that it was 'going to be a late decision' by the sponsor.

'Even if they don't renew, we will have more than replaced their [financial] commitment. The people we've known at Genesys are no longer there, and they're doing a major restructure of the business, so we don't even know if Genesys will exist by name, or whether it will be completely absorbed [by AMP]. But without them having come on board [in 2010], we wouldn't be around today.'

* * *

Nowadays, three quarters of Christie-Johnston's time is taken up with directing his team: he is the talent scout, coach, sports director, and mentor. The rest of the time he's trying to flog as many baked potatoes with curry, or whatever topping people want on top, as he can, so if there is a funding short-fall, he can keep the team going as it should, rather than cut corners.

'For Steve, it's probably about 50-50. He doesn't come away as much; he does more of the managerial side of the team. And we're lucky that we've got both our wives working in the [Praties] business; they're probably the ones that keep it afloat for us.'

How do they define success for the team? At the close of each season, what do they consider to be a good year?

'A good year for me and a good year for the team are probably slightly different. A good year managing the team is to make sure our sponsors are 100 per cent happy with their investment. And, to date, we've had mainly Australian sponsors, so to be the number-one team in Australia is important; it's important for them, and therefore it becomes a major priority for this team.

'They support our goal, which is to develop riders to the highest level. We can't race the highest-level races, but I sure can provide some talent to take that next level. So, for me, if I get a rider to take that next step, which we have in Nathan Earle, for example, then that's my goal ticked off. That's my personal goal, I suppose. But the job for us, as far as the NRS goes, is to be the number-one team in Australia each year, and I'd be disappointed if we don't achieve that in 2013.'

Other than the far more moneyed Australian Institute of Sport road and track cycling programmes, supported by taxpayers' dollars as well as Orica-GreenEdge benefactor Gerry Ryan, Christie-Johnston's team has placed more riders in road cycling's major league than any other team – all on the smell of an oily rag, relatively speaking.

'At the end of the day, I think you've got to get the right sort of guys. We've had a history of being able to develop guys and take them to that next level, and, as a result of that, we get a lot of riders wishing to join us,' says Christie-Johnston.

'We don't have the budget to pay many riders;

we've got a few guys we look after, but with the money we've got, we attract a lot of talent. And we spend a lot of time doing it. I've been following these NRS races for 15 years now, so there aren't many riders that I don't know. As I see them progress, I approach them… and we always seem to end up with a few solid, good guys.'

In his perpetual quest to find the next big thing, I wonder if Christie-Johnston purposely seeks those that fall outside the normal parameters of the AIS, but are nonetheless preternaturally talented.

'I think what we call the normal parameters of the AIS is difficult because the AIS can only take so many riders. It's not that some of these other people have fallen outside the parameters of the AIS, it's just that they can't take everyone. The thing with the AIS is that they grab who they believe are the athletes most likely to join the WorldTour and win medals for them. No one's got a crystal ball, so a lot of the time they take on riders, and they might find that they've picked up the wrong batch.

'I've found that there's been many a talented rider that hasn't been able to make it into that system because there was someone better on paper and he didn't get that opportunity. I try to use that to moti- vate the riders, to say: "Look, you've been overlooked for the moment. but you've got a long career ahead of you. Let's see what we can get out of this."'

When it looks as though his team will likely win

a fourth consecutive NRS teams title, does Christie-Johnston consider his team too good for domestic competition in Australia? It's competition that breeds success, is it not?

'I don't think it's necessarily that we're too good… I try to develop riders to get to that next level, and that has attracted good riders and has made us quite dominant. The reason why we're looking to go Pro Conti is because we want to expand our racing – and it's very difficult in Asia to get starts. We feel if we can afford to step up to Pro Conti, it would allow us to choose the races that we'd really like to do, rather than just getting knock-back after knock-back.

'We've been doing quite a few Asian races, but doing the same ones over and over again, and missing out on races like the Tour de Langkawi… We've never done it, and we'd love to do it. We've demonstrated on the climbs here in Australia that we're a good climbing team, and I've had quite a few guys that I really feel could've won that race, but we've never been able to do it, so it's about stepping up. And for a few of our senior riders it's maybe too late to take that next step to the WorldTour, so I'd like to have an additional budget to support them, to allow them to ride their bikes with a proper wage, for as long as they wish to.'

There's another, sadly darker, reason why the team is seeking Pro Continental status sooner rather than later. They want to compete in higher-ranked events that have more robust anti-doping measures. There's a feeling that among the races they do compete at within Asia, where regular doping controls vary between inadequate to non-existent (an example being the 2013 Tour of Borneo, ranked UCI 2.2), it's becoming the Wild East, making the playing field as flat as the monster climb up to the Genting Highlands. But, Christie-Johnston says, there is an upside.

'Some races you go to, you know you won't get a result. But it is still quite productive, having to race against that type of an athlete. If you're a C-grade rider and you're always riding against C-grade riders, it's hard to become a better rider. But some of the races we've gone to, we've got flogged, but at the end of the day, it's actually made some of our guys better riders. They might not get the results there at those races, but when they come back to other races, they start winning.

'The Tabriz Petrochemical team has always been… Their strength in Asia has always been phenomenal. And when they had two riders test positive at the Tour of Qinghai Lake – where we've raced for the past two years – it wasn't surprising to see that. We thought, great, that's going to fix it, they're going to be gone… and now they're back and they're back to being the number one team in Asia again.

'Unless I see a blood test done, I won't be convinced. I don't have trust. Like anyone else, when you have a team you've raced and they've gone positive, you lose trust in that team. But I think the good thing now is that there are a lot more teams that agree with us and are totally against it, and are actually forcing these guys out – even dealing with some of these situations on the road, themselves, to try to stop some of the results as best they can.

'But it's what we've had to deal with and what I've had to deal with for a long time. Dealing with it now is nowhere near the problem that it used to be; it is so much better. It's getting to the extent now where doping is so frowned upon by the riders, and that's fantastic. Before, it might not have been agreed with, but the riders weren't prepared to do anything about it. But have a look at some of the top people that are really getting out there and being a lot more boisterous than they ever were before. Before it was just silence.'

Whatever happens in the next few years, Christie-Johnston says, he will continue to operate out of his current abode in Hobart.

'I like to be close to home because the team's still about developing riders. I don't like to take them away for long periods of time; the biggest development of a rider comes through the training itself. Racing is where he gets recognised, but if he just races all year, you don't see progression in riders. It's the training camps we do, it's the structure in our training programmes that allow our riders to take that next step.'

When they made the jump to the WorldTour, the
five riders who've served under Christie-Johnston's
tutelage – William Clarke, Nathan Haas, Richie
Porte, Steele Von Hoff, and Nathan Earle (the latter
about to join Team Sky for 2014) – had an average
age of just under 25, which is around three to five
years older than those that made the grade via the
AIS. In the case of Haas, Porte and Von Hoff, they
were able to slip into the competitive swing straight
away. Does Christie-Johnston think, then, that some
get plucked too early?

'I think the AIS system is good and works for
some guys. But in my mind it doesn't work for all. A
lot of the time they have put them into something
they're not quite ready for, either physically or mentally. They've barely been into a decent team or environment that has given them any real understanding
about what that next step is.

'For us, we can introduce them to small blocks of
racing – we can send them to Asia for a week, or ten
days – and they can still come back into their own
environment, still feel a bit more normal, because
they've got a family life.

'For me, racing is a chance for riders to show their
ability – but training is the place where they make
their career. They need to put the miles in; they need
to do the training. And I think the support network
of being based at home enables them to do that
very well.'

* * *

More than once during 2012 Tour de France champion Sir Bradley Wiggins's breakthrough year, 'the kid from Kilburn' referred to Sky's head of performance support, Tim Kerrison.

The Australian is a former swimming coach, who worked at the Queensland Academy of Sport, and, from 2004 to 2008, adopted a similar role with the British swimming team, before eventually moving into cycling.

Following Wiggins's historic victory at *La Grande Boucle*, the British rider credited Kerrison for much of his success.

On the second rest day at the 2013 Tour, I, along with my colleague and friend Rupert Guinness, sat down with Kerrison in the Sky team bus to pick his brain for two hours about how the riders prepare better, train smarter, recover quicker, and thus race like no one's seen before in a Grand Tour.

With Christie-Johnston's pedigree as a swimmer, I couldn't help but notice parallels in the approach by both men – and, of course, their success.

'Well, first, I wouldn't compare myself to Tim Kerrison,' Christie-Johnston laughs, modest to the end. 'Tim's done everything in swimming, whereas I've done very little. But I could see, back from my days as a swimmer, that things were done totally differently compared to cycling.

'As a swimmer, I'd do two sessions a day. I'd start very early in the morning. I'd often have some core sessions, some stretching, and some gym work. And it was a complete, modularised system where you knew exactly what you were going to do before you got there.

'It's very different to the coaching standards in Australia in cycling. When I first jumped on a bike, I said: "Okay, where do I find a coach?" Everyone said: "Coach? What do you need a coach for? Just ride your bike." Then I said: "When I'm not riding my bike, what am I doing?" Their reply: "That's up to you; just ride your bike."

'So, swimming was miles in front of cycling. As far as the Olympics go, swimming's always been the number one sport in Australia, and they've always had that experience.

Cycling, traditionally – even in the days of [former national cycling coach] Charlie Walsh – was always about load, doing miles, and not doing a lot of extra work outside of cycling.

'With Sky bringing in someone like Tim, they brought in the coaching aspect and the discipline that the swimmers have always had, which is far more advanced.

'For Richie Porte and guys like Chris Froome, Tim brings a science to cycling. You just don't ride your bike all the time. There's a lot of things you can do when you're not riding your bike.'

* * *

Here's Andrew Christie-Johnston's recollection of how he managed to unearth the aforementioned quintet of talents who, if it wasn't for him, would likely have got away, and where he sees their *métier* in the WorldTour peloton.

RICHIE PORTE
(rode for Praties 2008-09, turned pro with Saxo Bank 2010, rode for Team Sky from 2012)

'Back in 2007, we were very committed to just having Tasmanian cyclists. And Richie, from the small amount of racing that I'd seen, seemed like a guy that was very disciplined, and his work ethic in a race was pretty impressive. You could see that he didn't really understand a lot of the racing, but as he came up through the grades, he was just so strong. He really went from a C-grade rider to an A-grade rider within races.

'And, once I recognised him as a guy with real promise, I started doing a lot more research into it, and found out a bit more about his history and what he'd done, and understood then he had already been an elite triathlete. So, for me, it was a no-brainer to invest some time and effort into him. He swam at the club where I knew all the coaches really well, so I knew his talent there. And I'd seen his bike splits, and I recognised that... If you have a look at what he actually did, he was pretty bloody talented, as a triathlete. He may not say that, but it was only his run leg that was his downfall, and I wasn't really worried about that side of it. He's only a small bloke; he [therefore] only takes small strides.

'As I was coaching him back then, you understand what a rider can actually do. In a race, you only get to see the result on how difficult the race is or what the circumstances are. But Richie's ability to train and do massive workloads was far bigger than any athlete that I've coached. By a long way. A big week is 1,000 kilometres, but he'd go and do 1,200, and handle that sort of thing very well.

'When you've got a guy that can do that – then do it again the next day – you know you've got an athlete who's very special. So, knowing that a Grand Tour rider needs to be someone that can actually do that workload and keep up that workload, yeah, I really did think he could go to that highest level. I was hesitant only in the way pro cycling was at the time, as a lot of Australian amateurs would be... As soon as we realised around the time Richie was getting involved that things were cleaning up, you could see he was competing very well, and that was very pleasing.

'Back then, around those years [he was with our team], his workload was just phenomenal. When we put him on those climbs in Tasmania – Cadel Evans had done the Tour of Tasmania and won a stage on Mount Wellington; I have all these times – and we had a look at what Richie could do, the fact that he could just destroy Cadel's times up those climbs was a pretty impressive feat. And Richie didn't just do this once – he did it on multiple occasions. And on one occasion he did it after a 200-kilometre ride.

'We had a rider in Richie who couldn't necessarily perform at his best in Australia because the type of racing he was doing back then was really limited to sprinter, punchy-type riders. So he looked good, but not brilliant. As soon as he got the opportunity to go to Italy to do races that did suit him, you could see straight away that he was going to get there.

'Most definitely, I think he's ready to be a leader at the [2014] Giro. There's no doubt the Tour has the attention of everyone, but you probably get looked after a lot better by your team. Everyone can forecast what's going to happen at the Tour, to some degree. So, I think that's going to be a difficult thing for Richie. But, at the end of the day, he's been there; he's already done the Giro, he's done the Tour… I think he's ready. I think he's got the maturity to do it. But have one bad day in a Grand Tour and your race is over.

'If he's decided that he wants to do it, then he'll be up there, for sure. I think he's pretty well rounded at this stage. But you're only as good as your team; if they relax at some point, and just drift back in the peloton at the wrong time, they'll get caught out. But he's got all the tools to do it – it's more about having a good enough team behind him. And I think that may be a challenge, because obviously their focus will be massively on the Tour. I don't think he needs to improve on anything, really. He needs luck, and you need to be on your game; you have to ride position. But he's proven he can do that.'

WILLIAM CLARKE
(rode for Praties 2008-10, turned pro with Leopard-Trek 2011, rode for Argos-Shimano 2013)

'Will comes from the middle of Tassie, half-way between Launceston and Hobart, in Campbell Town. He's a country boy, basically. There's not many people out there…

'He was a very gifted 800-metre runner. Like me, he was a Launceston Church Grammar School boy, so I knew him and I knew how talented he was through the running ranks. Due to injury, he wanted to get on the bike. We do a lot of handicap racing in Tasmania, and it shows the real strength of a rider.

'He's never going to be a prolific winner – he's just not going to be. He's a guy that's just heart. You tell him to do something and he'll do it, 110 per cent. And he's just massively strong. Every race that he does, whatever team he's on, he's the first guy they call on.

'So, he's always the first guy that might ride 100 kilometres on the front, and then, by two-thirds' distance of the race, he's already gone; his job's done. The thing with Will, though, is that he's not that comfortable in the bunch. I think he still needs to improve his bunch skills; he seems to get caught out in positions where he shouldn't. And he's a guy who never gets recognition – that's the biggest problem. When he changed to go to Champion System, in 2012, it was because 12 or so riders from his Leopard-Trek team had to lose their jobs due to the merger with RadioShack. He wasn't going to be bringing any UCI points with him, so despite being a really good worker, he was an obvious one to cut

'He did nearly 120 race days as a neo-pro at Leopard-Trek, and he was over-raced. You do 120 race days and it's a load for anyone, but Will's race days always involved a massive amount of time on the front. For a neo-pro, that's too much.

'He definitely wasn't managed well, and once it was recognised that [fellow Aussie] Stuart O'Grady was leaving Leopard-Trek to join Orica-GreenEdge, they weren't interested in Will. It was like, okay, just use him. No intention of re-signing him… They just abused him, really. I thought it would make him a stronger rider if he actually got through it, because once he had his rest, he would come out a stronger rider the following year.

'He came out as a stronger rider the following

year, but without a contract. If you're going to put
guys as neo-pros through that massive load, that is
okay if you have a plan for them. But they had no
plan for him, no intention to keep him. Going to
a team like Champion System, it was more of an
opportunity for him. But, racing like he had to, all
around the world – Champion System races in Asia,
races a bit in Europe, a bit in America – the amount
of travel that guy had to do was really, really difficult.
We caught up in about three races that overlapped
with Champion System, and he was just flogged.

   'He's going to be a very good *domestique*. And he's
an opportunist; if he's given an opportunist's job,
then he's quick – he's a very fast guy who could win
from small breaks.

   'His talent should be just riding in the front and
maybe the early part of a lead-out train. Not everyone in world cycling is going to get the result; they
have to accept they've got a role and do it well, and
they'll get paid well to do it. And when the opportunities come up, he can grab those. I hope that Will
does get a few in some of the smaller races, but the
time you get those opportunities is normally late in
the season, and by then you're pretty flogged and it's
difficult to get a result.

   'I speak to Will a lot, and, compared to, say, the
last two teams, he's actually really enjoying his time
at Argos-Shimano. He's in a good place, and very
happy. He gets along with the guys really well, and

I think that if he has the opportunity to stay there for longer, then he wants to be there because he's actually really enjoying it. And that's the first positive thing I've heard from Will in the last couple of years. He's found a place where he enjoys his job, and that will really make a massive difference in the next year or so for him. He'll probably turn out to be a guy like Mat Hayman, but I think that the difference with Will is that because he came to the sport quite late, he's going to take a few years longer to get to that sort of level.'

NATHAN HAAS
(rode for Praties 2009, Genesys Wealth Advisers 2010-11, turned pro with Garmin in 2012)

'I got to see Nathan when Tasmania took on the Australian programme for mountain biking. I did see what he did overseas, but I also went to some of the mountain-bike rounds [in Australia]. Actually, I put Nathan Earle into a mountain bike round that was in Hobart one year – just because he had a mountain bike – and that's when I first saw Haasy and recognised that he was pretty talented in some areas and maybe not totally suited to mountain biking. To me, he didn't ever seem skilful enough! On certain courses, he'd be really good, and on some of the technical courses, not so good. And World Cups are very technical, generally.

'On the road, he was someone who could climb quite well, but was also a very punchy rider. He had a good kick on him. And he's a bit of an all-rounder. So he time trials well, he climbs well, and he's quite quick. At the 2009 Tour of Tasmania, he raced for a local team that was put together for the mountain-bike squad, and that's where I got to see him. I think he won the 'king of the mountains' jersey. He was just aggressive – he was riding in every move he could get in. I thought: "Yep."

'In 2010, I actually told him I was very disappointed in his season because I knew how talented he was. I found out he was quite lazy in his training. He was at university and I think he was enjoying university life and trying to cycle as well. I said: "I can't tolerate this any more – if you want to be a cyclist, you need to defer your studies, get out of the university campus, and have a crack. If you wish to stay at university and on campus, then I don't want you on the team." Not that I was trying to get him away from his studies; it was that he was frustrating me with how talented he was, on the basis of doing little training... Doing ergo sessions because he'd been out partying, that sort of stuff. I just put it back on him and he said: "Yep, you're right – I'm going to give it a crack." I told him: "If you give it 100 per cent, I'll get 100 per cent out of you."

'Then I started coaching him. I brought him down to Tassie and spent a couple of months with him, and absolutely changed the type of rider he was. He lost all the weight; I had him three-and-a-half kilos lighter than he is now, even as a pro. And the amount of miles that he put in, I thought, "Right – now they're going to see the real Nathan Haas." And I could see it coming three months before he started going to these NRS tours. He'd put in the work that he hadn't done in other years.

'Now he had the talent, now he'd done the work – he was always going to be dominant, and yeah, I was pleased that he went out and had a great season. Of course, I really didn't think he'd win the Herald Sun Tour, but I knew that he had exceptional form going to the Tour of Tasmania, and I thought if he came out of the Tour of Tas' well, he'd give it a red-hot crack.

'Allan Peiper [then a Garmin sports director] contacted me not about Nathan Haas but about Steele Von Hoff, who had had so many wins in Australia that it caught the attention of quite a few managers.

'We chatted about Steele and Peiper said: "I'm interested in signing him. What do you reckon?" I told him that I thought he wasn't ready. Steele was quick enough to go and win some races early on, but he wouldn't get through the season. Then we got talking: "There's another rider that you may want to look at, though," I told him. "He's had a great season so far, but I think you'll be very impressed in the next couple of months." And

I mentioned Nathan Haas, and Peiper said: "No worries – I'll keep an eye on him."

'When he won the Tour of Tas', Peiper came back to me.

"'Just wait for the Sun Tour – I think he'll do very well," I told him.

'Halfway through the Sun Tour, Peiper said he wanted to talk, and by the time Nathan had won the race, although nothing had been signed, a deal was agreed upon.

'But then Saxo Bank made Haasy an offer as well, so he had two offers on the table. He could've just cut it and gone to Saxo Bank, but Nathan said to me: "No – I've given Garmin my word." And good on him, because I think at the end of the day, your word really should be your word.

'Haasy is more of an all-rounder – a bit like Philippe Gilbert or Simon Gerrans. He can get over a climb, and he can sprint, so to go down the path he's talking, it definitely suits the type of rider he is.'

STEELE VON HOFF

(rode for Genesys Wealth Advisers 2011, Chipotle-First Solar in 2012, turned pro with Garmin-Sharp 2013)

'In 2011, Steele was finishing his apprenticeship as a boilermaker when he was riding with us. He needed to get through June to finish it, so I said: "That's fine, mate, because I'll give you a programme that you

can manage with your 40-hour week doing boiler-
making, and we'll give you a very good base. Then,
after you've finished that, you're going to go into
a lot of races suited to sprinting." As soon as he
finished his apprenticeship, he came straight down
for six weeks to Tassie and prepared for the Tour
of Gippsland. I rented a house not far around the
corner from me, and put Steele and Haasy both up
together in that, making sure they trained together,
and that I had full contact with them.

'From that point onwards, he started winning
every sprint there was, really. But when the call came
from Peiper, who was interested in him because he'd
won 12 NRS races or something, it would have been
wrong of me to say that he was ready to turn pro,
because only two months previously he was a full-
time boilermaker. Whilst I knew that he had the
speed to get results, he didn't have the miles in his
legs to be able to continue with that. So Peiper
said: "Okay, we've got this under-23 development
squad – we'll put him in that, and maybe give him a
stagiaire [apprentice] role mid-season, with the intention of going pro in 2013." I said that'd be perfect; it
was exactly what he needed.

'Peiper then called me back: "Hey – he's not un-
der-23!"

"Yeah, I know – I told you that," I said, and so
Peiper basically said: "We're not an under-23 squad
any more; we're a development squad." So they

dropped the under-23 rule and just became a development squad! He got his opportunity as a *stagiaire*, impressed with what he did, and got the contract that he was probably going to get the year before. But it was more appropriate to wait that extra year to get the miles in his legs.

'I first heard about Steele when someone basically said to me, "Keep an eye on this guy." He was doing club races and some local stage races, but I saw him at the Melbourne to Ballarat one-day race and saw how bloody quick he was and thought, "Well, he's got heaps of speed, and I think in Australia he's got a very good opportunity to win stages."

'Again, I started looking at the results and some of the things that he did. I noticed he was into the recumbent-type human-powered vehicles (HPVs), where they go in those aero cockpits. His interest in that was that he was a welder, so he liked making his own. Then he decided, "Okay, well, I'm pretty fit, I might as well have a go at it."

'And in this one year, I noticed that the Uni of South Australia designed this really good HPV that was expected to win the world title in Adelaide. They thought, "Right, we've got it; we need to get a really good rider," so they put Jack Bobridge in there, thinking that, as one of the top cyclists in Australia, he would do a good job. Steele rocked up with his home-built one, lapped Bobridge in the race, and took the title.'

NATHAN EARLE
*(rode for Praties 2008-09, Genesys Wealth Advisers from
2010-12, Huon Salmon-Genesys 2013,
will turn pro with Team Sky 2014)*

'Like Richie, Nathan also comes from a background
in triathlon, and Richie definitely played a major
part in him joining Sky. Richie knows Nathan from
the early days, where he saw his talent and had to
work for Nathan – he had to take a back seat to him.
Richie always wanted to see him make that next step,
but you never want to see a guy take that next level
until he's actually ready. At the start of 2013, between
Richie and myself, we said, "Let's have a look at how
he goes for the next 12 months..." And then he
started winning a lot of races. So it's the ideal time
to turn pro.

'I'm not sure of the exact date, but his first problem was in 2010. He had a crash in training and broke
his kneecap, which wasn't diagnosed at first. It was a
micro-fracture, so what happened was underneath;
there was a whole lot of big bone that wasn't picked
up. He continued to ride. He had some X-rays; he
had pain but they said there was nothing wrong – just
a bit of tendonitis.

'When he got keyhole surgery done about five
months later, and they realised that there were some
bone fragments that weren't picked up, he'd nearly
cut his entire tendon away. So he had to have six

months off the bike to repair his tendon, then about another six months to get back to where he was.

'In 2011, we sent him to Italy, and straight away he showed some really good form. A WorldTour team was going to have a look at him at a race. It was Liquigas. Two days before that, he got hit by a car and broke his ankle. So, for Nathan, he's been plagued with unlucky crashes, and he just hasn't been able to put together a solid 12-month block anywhere without having major time off.

'When you're having six months off the bike at a time, it really does take a while to get back to where you were. And with Nathan, I always knew that if he could just have some luck – or not have bad luck – and put 18 months, two years, together, we would see the best of him.

'And that's what he's done: right from the start of 2013 and late last year, he put some solid results on the board and rocked up at races like the Herald Sun Tour with great form.

'I think he's like a Simon Gerrans. He can climb with someone like Gerrans, and he's as quick as him. And if he takes maybe another three kilos off in muscle mass, then he will be a phenomenal climber. He is a punchy rider; he can win from small bunch kicks, as he's done this year in Asia, and he's very hard to drop on the climbs. So I think that Nathan will be a work-in-progress for Sky. They will trim him down; when Richie left our team he still had that triathlete body-shape to him; just look at his arms now, and his upper body's nothing. Once Nathan gets like that, you'll see another guy who will climb like Porte. He'll be ideal for Sky on the climbs. He doesn't have the same time-trial pedigree as Richie, but I think he'll be a very solid worker for Sky on the climbs, and an opportunist in maybe some of the Ardennes Classics.

'To be a GC rider, he'd have to improve his time trialling. He's always thereabouts in the time trial; his numbers show that he could do all right, but he has this real problem about the concentration required for a time trial. It sounds a bit silly, but there's a lot of guys you think should time trial well who just don't. He needs to overcome those sorts of things, but at the end of the day, Sky will just put him to work in the hilly races. And once they recognise what they have, he'll be well suited to some of these smaller races that Richie's had a start in.

'He'll fit in at Sky, no problems. He's going to a team where everything is provided. They always know exactly what they're doing – and he needs that. It's the perfect place for him.'

Buoyed by the Olympic Games in his hometown of Sydney, **Anthony Tan** swiftly turned his back on a lucrative advertising career, melding journalism with experiences as a handy road racer that took him to Europe – briefly. He has covered the Tour de France since 2001, and is a cycling analyst for SBS Television Australia, the country's official broadcaster of the Tour.

7

Before the Tour de France, Laurent Jalabert was called by the French Senate to face questions about doping during his career.

Retrospective positive tests and the former world number one's ambiguous responses led to him losing his job as a pundit on French television.

As **Samuel Abt** explains, few people asked questions during Jaja's era, but, since the fall of Lance Armstrong, the past has been reappraised, with some inconsistent consequences.

DIFFERENT TIMES

BY SAMUEL ABT

A little more than a decade ago, maybe 2001 or 2002, I had lunch with an American rider (no, not Lance Armstrong) I had known for quite a while and had often interviewed. This time it was not an interview but more a social visit since I was passing through the town in Europe where he lived during the season. I was simply touching base with the rider, whom I will not identify, and was not taking notes nor using a tape recorder.

So it was chitchat – 'How's your form? What's your next race? Going back to the States any time soon?' – as we sat outside a café and had a sandwich and a glass of wine.

Near the end of lunch, I asked him about a rumour I'd heard: 'Are you working with an Italian doctor?'

His mood, until then relaxed, darkened. 'Why do you want to know?' he asked angrily. 'What are you implying?'

'Nothing,' I said. 'Just something I heard and wondered what it meant.'

'It means nothing,' he said. 'I'm not seeing an Italian doctor. If your question means, "Are you doping?" the answer is absolutely not. Never have, never will.'

He then suddenly remembered another appointment and left our table.

I didn't see him again until an early race the next season. When we ran into each other, I asked when we could get together for an interview about the races ahead.

'You'll have to see the team's press officer,' he said, aloofly. 'I'm pretty busy and maybe he can't fit you in.'

He walked off.

Puzzled by the new attitude of a rider I knew so well, I never did talk to the press officer. Nor did I ask the rider for an interview again; he was interesting and articulate, but not a star or a newsmaker, so, if he didn't need me, I didn't need him either as a source.

Still, I felt bothered to have lost touch with somebody I liked; not a friend exactly, since writers can't afford to have riders as friends, but, as I say, somebody I liked. Near the end of that season, I confronted the rider and asked him what had soured our relationship.

'You accused me of doping,' he replied. 'That's unforgivable. I told you I never doped.'

But, sadly, he had. He confessed after the US

Anti-Doping Agency's Reasoned Decision implicated him. A few years before we were having our lunch, and I was asking my aimless question, he had been seeing an Italian doctor and buying and using EPO.

In his confession, he apologised to fans, friends and fellow riders for letting them down. He disclosed no details or names. Those were different times, he insisted.

Indeed they were, in some ways.

* * *

A weird – very weird – rumour went around in the mid-1990s: Laurent Jalabert, it said, had needed to order new racing shoes because his old ones were now a size too small. What accounted for this growth in a man in his late 20s? The answer was, invariably, a sly smile.

Not that the reserved Jalabert gave that answer or any other. Nobody would have dared ask him. In those days, reporters didn't ask that sort of outlandish question; it was considered invasive of a rider's privacy in a sport built on casual fellowship, not the accusatory journalism that arrived with Lance Armstrong's comeback in 1999. Besides, Jalabert, whom everybody called 'Jaja', was the golden boy of the sport, and who would have wanted to believe a hint that he was doping?

Golden boy he surely was: the sport's top-ranked

rider in 1995, '96, '97 and '99. His list of victories in
one-day Classics was formidable: Milan-San Remo,
1995; the Tour of Lombardy, 1997; the Clásica San
Sebastián, 2001 and 2002; Flèche Wallonne, 1995,
1997; the Classique des Alpes, 1996, 1998; Milan-
Turin, 1997. He was the world time trial champion
in 1997 and the French road race champion in 1998.
Other victories included the Tour of Romandy, the
Critérium International, the Tour of the Basque
Country and the Tour of Catalonia. He finished first
in Paris-Nice from 1995 through 1997.

Jalabert's record in the Grand Tours was less
impressive: an overall victory in the Vuelta in 1995,
three stages in the Giro and four in the Tour de
France, where he was also points champion in
1992 and 1995 and top climber in 2001 and 2002.
Despite those polka-dot jerseys, he never excelled in
the loftiest mountains and so never finished higher
than fourth in the Tour.

He might have won many more of the spring
Classics but, after he broke in with the French
Toshiba team in 1989, he joined a Spanish team,
ONCE and rode for them from 1992 through 2000.

Apart from the Tour and Paris-Nice, ONCE
didn't often appear in French races, not least when
they shared the schedule with the Vuelta, which until
1995 was staged in late April and early May.

His breakout year was 1995, when he was 27.
In the 1994 Tour, he crashed heavily when riders

collided with a policeman taking a photograph of a mass sprint finish. Jalabert broke his jaw and both cheekbones and shattered his front teeth. He needed three hours of surgery and six weeks of recovery.

'That crash changed me,' he said in an interview then. 'Racing became more important. I might have lost everything and, without the bicycle, what would I have done?'

Before the crash, he was a moderately successful rider, and a good, if not great, sprinter. The next year he won an amazing 22 races and became number one in the sport. He was idolised in France.

'There are champions that everybody admires,' wrote the sports newspaper *L'Equipe* of Jalabert. 'They seem to come from another world, they have another dimension. And there are champions that everybody loves... because they've had their misfortunes, because they've had to earn their success, because, in addition to their talent, they resemble the rest of us.'

Typically for a man of so little flash, Jalabert chose a low-key news conference on a rest day during the 2002 Tour to announce that he would be retiring at the end of the season. He had left ONCE two years earlier and finished his career with Danish squad CSC. Thereafter he served as the French coach in the world championships from 2009 until 2013 and as a commentator for years with French television, where he was smart and incisive.

* * *

Jalabert had to retire as national coach after he was seriously injured by a car while on a training ride early in 2013. His break with the television channels was starker. Just before the Tour set off in Corsica, he was named in a French Senate report into doping in sports.

The Senate committee later identified 18 riders in the 1998 and 1999 Tours de France, including Jalabert, who retroactively failed drug tests for EPO and 12 whose samples were suspicious.

The 1998 Tour was the one nearly scuttled by the Festina Affair – a massive drug bust that included police searches of team hotels, rider strikes led by Jalabert and the protest withdrawal of several Spanish teams, including ONCE.

At least in France, Jalabert's name was the big one on the Senate list. Marco Pantani, who won that Tour, is dead now, a victim of cocaine in 2004, and Jan Ullrich, who finished second, finally admitted doping earlier in 2013. Around Jalabert, there remains an ambiguity that he helped spin in 50 minutes of testimony.

While he denied under oath that he knowingly used illegal performance-enhancing drugs, he added: 'I can't firmly say that I've never taken anything illegal. The team doctor took care of us, for our recovery, but we didn't really know what it was. A relationship with doctors based on mutual trust was established, so we didn't ask questions.

'At no time did I go looking for a doctor or anyone like that with the goal of improving my performance,' Jalabert continued. 'I never spent a single euro – rather, a franc; it was a while ago – to go to see a doctor or buy any banned products. But it's true that I was in these teams and I was looked after… And now, can I say today that it was illegal? I can't be sure. I can't be sure either that it was entirely legal.'

He named no names. He applauded what he called changes in the sport's culture.

How did all this go down with French media and fans? Thus far, no problem. The French have too few sports heroes – especially a rider who twice won a Tour stage on Bastille Day, the national holiday – to discard Jalabert.

Another former rider named in the Senate report, Jacky Durand, as well as Richard Virenque – not named but who had already confessed to using EPO – have kept their announcing jobs with Eurosport. Expect Jalabert to be back on television soon.

As people are saying, it was so long ago. And, they invariably add, those were different times.

Samuel Abt is the first American to be awarded the Tour de France medal for service to the race. He began writing about bicycle racing in 1977 for the *International Herald Tribune* and the *New York Times* and covered the Tour 32 times. Now retired as a newspaperman, he lives in France.

8

Corsica's magnificence was beamed around the world during the opening weekend of the 100th edition of the Tour de France.

The success of the *Grand Départ* there was clear.

However, a week before the start, the signs were not so promising.

Owen Slot discovered pungent cheese, a high murder rate and apathy towards the Tour's arrival. Though awed by the island's beauty he wondered whether Corsica was up to the task.

ISLAND MENTALITY

BY OWEN SLOT

The heat. He seemed to be inhaling heat into his lungs as if he was sucking it up through a straw. He tried to take his mind off it, thus triggering an internal conversation he knew so well: concentrate on the pedals, find a rhythm, ignore the pain, focus on the rhythm to block out the pain.

This was only stage two. Stage two of the Tour de France. It shouldn't hurt this bad. Not here. He wondered if the other riders had seen it in his face, if they had clocked his dilemmas so revealingly early in the race.

When the mountain is starting to win the battle, you instinctively look for shards of hope, anything to remind you that the mountain doesn't win. Always conquer the mountain. But on stage two of the 2013 Tour, three categorised climbs in quick succession, towards the highest point that Corsica would take them, had struck a collective blow. The mountain was winning.

The signpost helped, though. It wasn't official Tour de France signing – just a wooden post with the information carved into the weathered pine. Two-and-a-half kilometres to the summit of the Col de Vizzavona. Its information, however, was one-and-a-half kilometres short.

By now the group had started to splinter. He tried to hold the wheel in front, but slid gradually backwards and then it was gone. On his own, he searched again for that rhythm, but he was struggling. His bike swayed as he raised himself out of the saddle, slightly too laboriously shifting his weight, left and right, to maintain some sense of momentum. Still, the road climbed relentlessly. Where was the finish?

And then, finally, half a kilometre from the crest of the Vizzavona, he did the most extraordinary thing. He saw it ahead of him and instantly his mind was made up. He reached the café at the side of the road and there he came to a halt. He then unclipped from his pedals, leant his bike against the fencing, sat down and ordered himself a beer.

Pietra is the local brew. Strong, amber, brewed from a mix of malt and chestnut flour. When he had finally drained his glass, he declared firmly, 'That was the best beer of my life.'

The rider in this story is Gerald Tremlett. He is a decent athlete, though unlikely ever to make a living as a rider. Not at the age of 45. By profession he is world-class, instead, at producing and selling mattresses.

To complete the tale of the stage, Gerald eventually

remounted, knowing that the feed zone was only 15 minutes away – a beautiful stretch of road and almost entirely an adrenalin-boosting downhill high. At the feed zone, we all unclipped and we didn't move for an hour. We gorged ourselves and basked in the sun that was previously our enemy. It was bliss.

Uncle Mike – a doctor who insists on riding in a green construction worker's jacket, and is 57 – then explained to Gerald that, on the Vizzavona, he had bonked. All riders can bonk, even the pros, he explained. Gerald felt still better for that. And then, eventually, we all rode on together, harmoniously as a chain gang, all the way into Ajaccio. It was bliss.

This was exactly a week before the Tour de France. A different event, called the Tour de Force, which rides the exact same route in the exact same timescale a week before the Tour itself.

But I won't bore you with any more of our two-wheeled travelogue. You don't want to know about the climbs we rode, how we felt higher than the summits themselves, how we so treasured our own mild victories over eight categorised climbs and felt slightly liberated, deliciously cut off from our normal lives and, curiously, so alive. If you have a bike and love it, you no doubt recognise all these sentiments.

What you will not know is that, a week ahead of the biggest event ever to come to this rough jewel of an island, Corsica felt quiet, unstirred. It was so quiet, you might hardly have known it was

coming. There was no drum roll of anticipation.
Which seemed strange.

Some basic background. As if you could possibly have been unaware, this was to be the 100th
staging of the Tour de France. It was a massive deal.
The Tour's marketing department had long been in
overdrive. A deluge of history books flooded the
bookshelves. The 100th Tour was given a 100th Tour
logo. This was so big, we were informed, that every
single living cyclist ever to have completed an entire
Tour de France had been invited to the finish in Paris
(apart from Lance Armstrong, though that's another
story). Yet here at the start, they were playing it so
damned cool it was as if they had hardly noticed.

Some more background: there are 96 *départements*
in France. That is the way the country is geographi-
cally and administratively divided. The Tour had previously travelled through 94 of them. The only two
never to have been graced by the peloton were the
two that comprise Corsica. Of course, the Tour had
also been abroad. It is a confident traveller, regularly
zipping in and out of its neighbouring countries; it
had been across the water to London and Dublin.
There was even long-held talk of taking the race to
the United States. But Corsica? Never a sniff.

The closest Corsica had come to the Tour de
France was, arguably, when Tommy Simpson bought
some property on the island before his death. Or
maybe the fact that Jacques Anquetil's daughter runs

a hotel in the north, a few miles from Calvi where stage three would finish.

And yet here was Corsica, a week away from losing its virginity, and there was no sign whatsoever of the knees trembling, the islanders readying themselves to shriek with high-voltage final fulfilment.

And my, how on the mainland they would have scoffed. They know the island for its high murder-rate, for the passionate freedom fighters they do not understand, for the inhabitants' natural *froideur*.

They also didn't much rate Corsica's chances of pulling this whole thing off. Corsica doesn't organise big events. No one trusts them to do so. Certainly not a whopping event like the Tour de France. The Tour's history is about expansionism, sometimes referred to as gigantism. Big is good.

A week before the *Grand Départ*, Gerald and I took a walk around Porto-Vecchio – the *Grand Départ* town. Very fishing-village quaint, very quiet. Not even a string of bunting across the main street.

'Is this it?' Gerald asked rhetorically. 'Not exactly *Grand*, is it?'

We sat out at a bar in front of the port. 'Where, exactly are they starting from?' we asked a waiter. He shrugged and gestured vaguely. He didn't know.

We then wandered up the steep track to the old town – and the old town was glorious. Cobbled, packed tight, wafer-thin streets, atmospheric, wall-to-wall with bars and pizzerias. We loved the old town. But the Tour wouldn't be going through the old town. Too steep, too narrow.

That was when Gerald recalled Corsica as he had first known it. In *Asterix in Corsica*, he recounted, the islanders are notable for producing cheese so pungent that when it catches fire, it explodes and blows up a pirate ship. They are also portrayed as lazy, in love with their afternoon siesta, and for taking honour and respect so seriously that pretty much the only thing that will stir them from their siesta is when their honour and respect require defending and they have the opportunity to have a fight.

This all somehow seemed to fit. *Corse Matin*, the daily paper, had actually started to acknowledge that the Tour de France was on its way, yet a large part of its coverage tended to be given over to detailed maps of road closures, as if the event wasn't the greatest race on earth and more like some infernal building project. Recent stories had also included the one about the ferry ports threatening to go on strike during the Tour. And the one about the opinion polls which recorded that one in five Corsicans declared that they'd be happier if the Tour never came here and left them to their blissful remoteness instead.

This news may have been comparatively dry for *Corse Matin*, which benefits from being able to report on internal feuding bloodier even than its more notorious neighbours, Sicily and Sardinia. Indeed, nowhere in Europe has a murder rate higher than Corsica. Traditionally, this has been a falling-out between rival clans and gangs. Peppered throughout its history, Corsica has had pockets of punchy freedom fighters, traditionally strongest at the island's central town of Corte, whose cause has drifted towards terrorism. But it is maybe typically dysfunctional of Corsica that the cause of autonomy has been so ineffectively waged that at one point there were two sets of freedom fighters who ended up killing not the French overlords, but each other.

More recently, *Corse Matin* had been able to indulge itself on a spate of assassinations that were traced back to young, organised criminals with a cold eye on profiting from developing the island's tourism sites. The Corsican political elite is at least agreed on the fact that its island's beauty is its USP and that such development should be discouraged. Thus, Dominique Bucchini, the Corsican Assembly President, had explained: 'Pressure is put on mayors to grant planning permission. If they prevaricate, they find that their cars have been torched, or a bomb is set off near the mayor's office. And then it finally comes to a bullet in the head.'

With all this in my mind, I spoke to Marie-Hélène Djivas. Djivas does not come from Ajaccio or Corte or Calvi, or even Porto-Vecchio. No, it tells us quite a lot about Corsica that the supremo appointed to a massive role – to persuade the Tour to come here and then to manage their stages – is not Corsican at all. To avoid factions, divisions, or accusations of favouritism, they shipped in Djivas from Nice.

They gave her a preposterously long-winded, politically-worded job title, too. Djivas, instead, became known locally just as 'Madame Tour de France'. When I addressed her thus, her attractive blushing was rather splendid.

I asked her why, in 99 Tours de France, had the race never come here? Is it because Corsica is seen as too small? Or is it because Corsica is seen as too inferior? Or is it because of mainland snobbery and the belief that Corsicans can't be trusted to organise their darling bike race? Is it because the Tour is a sitting-duck target for political statements? Is it somehow tied up with murder rates and terrorism? Or is it just the pungent cheese?

No. None of that, Djivas said with a you'll-never-believe-it roll of the eyes. 'When I took the job,' she said, 'I found the Tour de France dossier was empty.' In other words, this wasn't a French problem but a Corsican one. In recent years, she explained, Corsica hadn't even submitted a proposal to stage the Tour because Corsicans were so divided they couldn't agree what their proposal should have in it.

Of the four main cities, two are politically left, two are right, and then there is Corte, the independence stronghold, in the middle. Djivas explained: money was the problem. Who would pay? Who would profit? For the right to host three stages and the *Grand Départ*, the Tour organisers wanted €3.5 million. Where would that come from? That's an argument before you have started.

An unlikely by-product of the 2013 Tour de France, then, is that it delivered a political rarity: Corsican unity. Instead of letting the factions fight in the traditional way, the *Collectivité Territoriale*, the island's umbrella body for which Djivas was working, put up the money and ran the whole affair. This was good for everyone; even the ethically challenged property developers could see that this might work as a kind of advertisement for the tourist industry they were so blood-thirstily keen to exploit.

It was with all this in mind that Gerald, Uncle Mike and I, along with our large peloton of Tour de Force riders, made our own grand départ from Porto-Vecchio exactly seven days before the pros – and the three days we shared were about as stunning as any of us had dared hope. We rather liked the occasional reminder that we were in small-time Corsica: the occasional whopping pothole, the bridge whose construction hadn't yet been completed, the unscheduled stop half-way up a category-three climb because a goat herd had decided to cross the road in front of us.

The three Corsica stages comprised 514 kilometres of which maybe only a 40-kilometre stretch into Bastia on stage one could not audition as a cinematic backdrop. By the end of day one, there was a

collective high all round which would never be shift-
ed by Gerald's bonking on day two. And then came
day three, and that jaw-dropping stretch around the
Calanques de Piana that the TV cameras would fall in
love with a week later, which was best of all.

Thus did three days on a bike completely shift
perceptions. We were in love with Corsica, whatever
the merits of its cheese.

Thus it was, at the end of 514 hard but brilliant
kilometres and with a heavy heart, that in Calvi I
bade farewell to Gerald, Uncle Mike and the Tour
de Force peloton. They would continue on to Nice
and the mainland adventure. I would send my bike
back home to London, collect a hire car and drive
back to Porto-Vecchio, back to the start, to cover the
same territory a second time, not as a rider but as a
journalist.

I smiled when I hit the Porto-Vecchio road that
the Tour would follow. Now, only four days, before
the start, Corsica seemed at last to be awaking to the
reality that the Tour was coming. Strings of bunting
were being hung across roads, teams of workers were
tidying up the roadsides. Flowers were being planted.
All so gloriously last-minute.

I wondered, too, if the Tour de France would
work the same perceptional change on Corsica's
army of doubters. And I kind of chuckled when I
was back at the start and reacquainted with the unmistakable littleness of it all. For the grand *Grand*

Départ of the 100th Tour, was quaint, village-y Porto-Vecchio some kind of ironic joke?

And then we had the Tour proper's day one – and the Orica-GreenEdge bus got stuck – and it seemed that Corsica's reputation was sealed. And again, on the mainland, my, how they must have laughed.

In the inevitable search for a culprit, some people blamed the Orica bus driver, some blamed ASO, the organisers. And many simply generalised and agreed that Corsica was the problem. Too small, too little know-how, the Tour was too big, the Tour should never have come here, this was an experiment that hadn't worked.

But stage two would be Corsica's comeback. The Tour wheeled through Corte and no one died. No bomb went off. They hadn't completely conformed, though. All along the road, daubed in white paint on the tarmac, were the letters FLNC – the National Liberation Front of Corsica – yet not even an angry firecracker gave voice to the message. From Corte, the road rose, up to the three categorised climbs, past the bar where Gerald had his beer, past the roadside site of our one-hour lunchtime picnic, and onto a cracking finish in Ajaccio where Jan Bakelants, the Belgian, survived just metres ahead of the pursuing pack.

As if it were possible, stage three would be even better. Already, the TV pictures had fallen in love with the landscape, but stage three would take it to another level. Somehow, the peloton negotiated the worst stretch of potholes, up the third-category climb where the goat herd had intervened a week before, and then into a long stretch of high, winding cliff-edge road that was reminiscent of the best of Cape Town.

The denouement in Calvi was another nail-biter, and by the time Simon Gerrans had edged a bunch finish, the Tour had had three different winners and two different yellow-jersey-wearers in three days. It had also not followed tradition by squeezing a sequence of sprint stages into its opening exchanges. It had dispensed with the accepted formula; it had conquered new territory.

From Calvi, we evacuated Corsica; most of the Tour de France circus would travel to Nice on over-night ferries. On my boat, there were team staff from many of the teams, there were large numbers of media and large numbers of cycling fans. There was also an unmistakable if weary kind of joy.

Corsica had been tough, long and logistically challenging. But it had also been rather special. Some asked a different kind of question: not 'What on earth is the Tour doing here?' but 'Why on earth hasn't it been here before?' It is not as if I conducted a survey, but the large majority on that boat seemed to think it had been a proper success.

Really, a success. The media reports over coming days would agree. One of the winners in that first week was the island itself. Small, inferior, incapable, divided, murderous Corsica had taught us that the Tour does not have to be gigantic.

The Tour has a simple formula: the best bike riders in the world racing hard in Arcadian landscapes is both beautiful and compelling. Which is how it feels for us lot in the amateur peloton, too. The Tour does not need size - the Tour doesn't need to go to New York. It can go back to Porto-Vecchio instead.

Owen Slot is chief sports reporter for *The Times*. He has three times won Sports Reporter of the Year and three times Sports Feature Writer of the Year. He has written five books, two of which were romantic comedies for which the film rights somehow remain unsold. As a bike rider, 2013 was his annus mirabilis, though despite the earnest efforts of sports psychs, he still descends rather gingerly.

9

Fool fans once, shame on you.
Fool fans twice, shame on them.

Klaus Bellon Gaitán assesses the
fallout from Lance Armstrong's
confession and wonders whether
some fans and commentators
have taken the adage too literally.

When Nairo Quintana won the
Tour of the Basque Country, it
prompted questions from a pair
of sceptics on American TV.

But is blindly questioning every
outstanding performance as bad
as the previous trend of taking
everything at face value?

OUT OF NOWHERE

BY KLAUS BELLON GAITÁN

DRAMATIS PERSONÆ

Steve Schlanger: American sports commentator who has worked on-air doing play-by-play for 'close to 30 sports' including hockey, basketball, golf, baseball, American football, alpine skiing and cycling. According to Schlanger's biography on a website that sells his services as a motivational speaker, 'The signature features of his broadcasting style are insightfulness coupled with a quick wit and sharp sense of humor. Key ingredients to his success are perseverance and ingenuity, as he has worked both hard and smart to achieve his success.'

Todd Gogulski: Retired professional cyclist who raced with American domestic teams Coors Light, Subaru-Montgomery, Crest and Lowenbrau. He retired from racing in 1992 and began doing live announcing at US races in 2006. Three years later he joined Universal Sports Network as a cycling commentator and pundit.

**April 6, 2013: Universal Sports Network's live
post-race coverage of the Tour of the Basque
Country, after the final time trial where Nairo
Quintana finished second to Tony Martin, and
won the race overall.**

Steve Schlanger: ... And because it was so surprising today, let's face it, we live in a day and age where
you can't bury your head in the sand any more [...]
no one gets the benefit of the doubt any more. And
when you have a surprising result like this from a
guy who comes out of nowhere to do this good in
a time trial, I think it's only fair to ask the question
about substances and if they're still in play.

Todd Gogulski: You have to Steve, uh, it's an ugly
thing to think about, it's something that I hope
doesn't exist with Quintana, but this was a ride that
no one could have expected. Now, to his credit,
we've seen him climbing very well in the last few
weeks. Two summit-finish wins. Incredibly good
climbing. We've seen him descending well in the
rain in this race as well as last year. To put that
together into a time trial like this... It makes you
wonder. It makes you ask the question, and I
certainly hope he doesn't get busted [...]

Steve Schlanger: Let's be clear. We're not accus-
ing him of anything, but it would be irresponsible,

considering everything that's happened over the last six months, not to ask the question.

Todd Gogulski: The question needs to be asked, and there's no way for us to know. There's absolutely no way for us to know, but certainly cycling fans will have to wonder: did he do that on his own, or did he have some kind of help?

Steve Schlanger: For now, he's the champion...

'Out of nowhere.' I heard the phrase, and my lips tightened up in anger – no small feat considering the bulky and uncomfortable adult braces that grace my teeth. My mood didn't change much for the remainder of the post-race commentary.

By the end of the broadcast, the inside of my lips were fused to my braces, so I had to peel the two apart like the worn zipper on an old backpack, further adding to my anger.

It was that phrase, 'out of nowhere', along with the subtext that came with it, and the fact that this was being said under the guise of being 'responsible' that troubled me. But the more I thought about it, the more I realised that there wasn't subtext at all; it was a clear accusation, along with several reasons as to why Movistar's Nairo Quintana, winner of the Tour of the Basque Country, was not to be trusted.

For some, the whole exchange between the

commentators, and the use of that phrase in particular, could have been dismissed as another bit of meaningless banter in a sport where riders 'dance on the pedals', own 'suitcases of courage' and experience more 'elastic snaps' during races than I do when trying to fit into undersized, Italian-made cycling clothing.

But I couldn't let it go. Instead I sat there, teeth, braces and lips fused into one, staring at the TV screen in anger. I felt a certain emotional contagion among fellow Colombian orthodontic patients like Sergio Henao, Carlos Betancur, and Esteban Chaves, our emotions converging, as their mouths would surely pucker up in outrage as they heard about these comments as well. With that, my emotions went from being dominated by a rather pedestrian type of patriotism, to an imagined telepathic bond among Colombians undergoing orthodontic treatment. In other words, I had gone from irrational nationalistic pride to just plain irrational.

So was my vision clouded by the mere fact that Quintana, like me, is Colombian? Possibly. Sports, after all, have managed to awaken a patriotic streak in me before, something I'm not necessarily proud of. But there was also the issue of the commentators being so uninformed that they honestly found his performance to be so unlikely as to make a point of questioning its validity. Was it really that strange that a Colombian climber who has excelled from a young age, one with relatively strong time trialling abilities, could have won the Tour of the Basque Country? The closing time trial in that race was a technical affair, and included short pitches as steep as 12 per cent – ideal for a climber like Quintana, who won the Tour de l'Avenir in 2010, the Vuelta a Murcia and the Route du Sud in 2012, and came to prominence with a mountain stage win that same year at the Critérium du Dauphiné. On that day, Quintana managed to ride away from the very best in the sport, including the then all-conquering Bradley Wiggins. This from a rider who came out of Colombia Es Pasion (now 4-72 Colombia) – the only team in Colombia with an internal biological passport and testing programme, a team with such a strong and unrepentant anti-doping ethos that they've become reviled by many in Colombia. It's a squad led by men like Ignacio Vélez, business advisor to the team, and Luis Fernando Saldarriaga, technical director, whose stubborn stance on the matter led them to use up a substantial amount of their team's budget on testing in the name of clean sport, and in order to not risk sullying their country's name with a doping positive.

Quintana would later touch on this very subject while speaking about his Colombian team's stance during an interview with Carlos Arribas from the Spanish daily *El Pais*.

'It's a team made up of great people, who have fought tirelessly against doping. They have a double bio-passport within the team, and they have a real belief in education... Saldarriaga always told us about his path, a hard one, versus a fast one filled with cheating. Everything was perfectly controlled. We had no pressure to win; they simply let us grow naturally, and created a path for us accordingly. They don't give their riders injections of any kind. All vitamins and supplements are done orally. I've never taken an injection, and I intend to keep it that way.'

Quintana's blood values from that team played a part in his signing with Movistar.

The more I thought about Nairo's past, the more my lips and face started to tighten up in anger again. But then I started to see the issue from a different angle. Endlessly defending any rider is a fool's game (whether said defence is based on fact, belief, patriotic hubris, or anything else). In part, because in doing so, we often miss the bigger picture, and thus lose our ability to examine the sport and its current mood as a whole. This, I feel, is far more meaningful than simply sitting at home angrily looking at a TV screen as commentators fill on-air time before a commercial break. How so? Allow me to explain.

A BINARY APPROACH IN A POST-OPRAH ERA

The phrase 'out of nowhere', and its common use in today's cycling parlance, has little to do with men like Quintana. In fact, its use reveals more about those who use it, and about the Zeitgeist of cycling in the post-Oprah confession era.

As I see it, 'out of nowhere', along with 'not normal', introduced by Tyler Hamilton in his book *The Secret Race*, and now the title of a report by Antoine Vayer, a coach and performance analyst, have become a quick and easy way to express disbelief in someone's performance, while hiding behind coded language that avoids outright accusations. This would be understandable enough if it were not also a way for commentators to feign being responsible broadcasters, and endear themselves to their listeners (much as they did when the opposite point of view was popular). In doing so, they come off as our brave ambassadors, agents of change who are saying what needs to be said in a turbulent time. However, such scepticism is meaningless and uninformed.

You see, we live in a time when even the most selectively lucid and casual cycling fans know the details about how the sausage is made (or at least how it was made ten years ago). Fans, pundits and commentators alike have drifted from the camp of the faithful toward total scepticism, and with good reason. But in a world where absolute truths and certainties are prized over reality's often-murkier waters (which tend to come in one of several shades of grey), many have unknowingly chosen to rely on binary logic instead.

In other words, if what they believed before

was wrong, then the opposite must be true. If their beloved icons were holy, clean and could possibly walk on water if asked to before, then in the face of their profound disappointment, only the complete opposite can be believed. It's a line of reasoning that is so astoundingly simplistic and flawed that George Costanza, the hapless character in the TV show *Seinfeld*, once took it on as a way to improve his miserable life. The idea is first introduced to George by Jerry Seinfeld's character, who sees where his normal reasoning has gotten him in life. It's ludicrous, and perfectly suited for a half-hour sitcom. And yet, many have – unknowingly – taken it on as a war-cry in real life.

Making matters more difficult is the fact that actual doubt is not only healthy, but also necessary in these matters. We certainly could have used more of it in the past, but its current iteration is shortsighted at best. We have arrived at it with the same blind reasoning that led many not to question matters in the past (it's worth mentioning here that the reasons for not questioning or defending in the past were many, and sometimes included blind patriotism).

But behind the current bravado in the voices of many pseudo-sceptics today, one can still detect the same emotional absolutism that was visible in their blind faith before, peeking out from behind, making the drastic change in both discourse and tone seem at once foolish and predictable. In fact, the mood swings of a hormonal teenager seem laughable by comparison, but such is the state of cycling today.

Scepticism is wielded as confidently as absolute faith is by some zealots, perhaps because it's the most reasonable and acceptable doctrine that a cycling fan can hope to experience today. It might also be the closest we can come to truth, or at least feeling like we know truth. As a result, doubt is a comfortable and familiar feeling. This, in turn, means that those who still believe are treated like relics of days long passed. They are seen as fools who have yet to be proved wrong, as everyone else digs their heels in the sand, substituting one seemingly irrefutable set of beliefs for another.

But why has this culture of doubt become so prevalent within cycling? Part of it, no doubt, has to do with the sheer amount of work that is necessary in doing due diligence, checking the *palmarès* and backgrounds of 200 riders from multiple nationalities. Perhaps it's asking for too much, though I'd gladly settle for anyone who at least knows about riders with major victories in the past, as well as the terrains in which they excel. But there's something else going on here. There's the foolish human need of feeling like we're in on a secret (yet another aspect of adolescent reality that follows us into adulthood like the barking dog that chases us on an otherwise leisurely bike ride). So suspicion becomes an easy way to feign enlightenment, as doubt goes from being a weapon for enquiries to a shield for uninformed cowardice.

Express excitement or interest, even to a limited degree, about a rider, team or race, and watch the binary sceptic's engine kick in.

'Oh, you think that team's clean? Ha-ha… I believed once upon a time, too. You'll learn soon enough, young grasshopper.'

In a quick one-two punch, we've been put in our place and their logic, reasoning and intellect has been shown as supreme – often with little factual information at play. The believer is the fool – a child who still waits for Santa and the tooth fairy to show up. In other words, the person who nodded along to Armstrong's 'I'm sorry you don't believe in miracles' speech after his 2005 Tour de France victory.

Suspicion becomes an intoxicatingly easy way to simulate sophistication or greater insight. And to be perfectly honest, like most cycling fans, I often find myself on both sides of the binary divide. I'm the believer at times; I remain the wide-eyed kid who first watched and listened to the Tour de France in 1984. But then, just as quickly as Mario Cipollini would retire from a mountainous Tour de France stage, I begin to doubt. I, too, begin to brandish my scepticism, shaking my head in disbelief. But I still want to enjoy myself, if only cautiously so.

This shift in emotions – and the reasoning behind it – is unlike anything that fans of other sports experience. It makes for an uncomfortable viewing experience, but such are the times in which we live. Sport, often a vehicle for very deep and real human drama, now requires something from cycling fans that seems highly unusual: the ability to suspend disbelief.

VALUE AND IMPACT

What is the value of scepticism when it comes from the same vacuous place as blind faith, and when its most significant result is the ability to retreat to a now popular and comfortable moral high ground? In other words, is this the kind of discernment that will help cycling turn a corner and advance, or is it as vacant and meaningless as the blind faith that preceded it? I don't know about you, but I'm really leaning toward the latter.

It's with this in mind that I realise the source of my frustration in all this. My anger upon hearing those comments about Quintana didn't come about because of my kinship to the man (or the flag-waving patriotism that comes with it, of which I admit I'm guilty). It also didn't come from some blind faith and belief in that man or his past. It came about because I believe wholeheartedly that the comments came from an empty place, and represent a bigger issue. Scepticism – even in hefty doses – is not only good, but essential in situations like the one cycling faces today. We need doubt, and all the journalistic enquiries that may come from it. But in a sport that was largely started by newspapers to increase readership, that often seems like too much to ask for. So instead, we are left with the voices of commentators and fans clawing their way up to this fictitious moral high ground, under the guise of rigorous and informed disbelief.

As with much of the discourse around cycling today, the commentators' opinion about Quintana showed how one emotion and reality have been seamlessly replaced by another, and we are left wondering where all this tough talk (meaningless or not) on the subject was years ago. So in a sense, the exchange between commentators at the end of the Tour of the Basque Country best exemplifies where much of the dialogue around professional cycling stands today: we've willingly traded in the possibility of having meaningful discourse for the comfort of perceived certainty. A pity, considering that we'd like to know the truth, and that many riders deserve a better-informed environment to race in as well. We want to know, and we should be sceptical. But answers will never come from such empty rhetoric.

Fool fans once, shame on you. Fool them twice, shame on them. Fool them 84 times (give or take a few), and they'll simply invert their logic endlessly, in the hope that they'll never get fooled again.

As for me, I'll simply try to wade in the murky

waters that lie between absolutes, nursing the wounds in my inner lips and hoping that I don't have to pry them apart from my braces yet again. But I know what the current mood in cycling is, and I know that another race is always around the corner.

And sadly, I'm beginning to feel my face tighten up in anger once again.

Klaus Bellon Gaitán was born in Bogotá, Colombia, and his family emigrated to the United States when he was 12 years old. He did not get orthodontic treatment during his teens due to his family's financial hardships, but also because he was stubborn, and didn't want to look foolish while having braces as a teenager. This resulted in him looking foolish while having braces well into his 30s. His writing has been published in *Road*, *Peloton*, *Bicycle Times*, and *Cycle Sport*. Klaus also publishes his own blog, *Cycling Inquisition*, and is a contributor to *Manual For Speed*.

10

What are the qualities that make a great bike race so great?

Edward Pickering explores the different ingredients that combine to make a memorable event and comes up with his own list of essential elements for a great race.

WHAT MAKES A GREAT RACE?

BY EDWARD PICKERING

The great lie about professional cycling is that it is always exciting. Actually, bike racing exists on a spectrum which runs all the way from moribund to exhilarating.

It's a lie propagated by fans, media and vested interests in the sport. Nobody wants to be the one to point out that while sport is advertised and marketed as an exciting experience, sometimes bike races can be the two-wheeled equivalent of the nil-nil draw. Granted, if your starting point is that you like bike racing, even watching the duller races still has value. But for every 1989 Tour, there's a 2012 Tour. For every Paris-Roubaix, there's a Vattenfall Cyclassics. For every edge-of-your-seat tactical battle, there's a long, flat sprint stage in the second week of the Vuelta a España.

It's not easy to define exactly what makes a good bike race. If it could be bottled, organisers would help themselves to a magnum of the stuff and sprinkle it liberally over their event. It's also an extremely subjective question. Different people have different ideas about what makes a good race. There are five distinct constituencies in professional cycling: fans, media, riders, teams/sponsors and race organisers, and each has different criteria for judging races. For a sponsor, a good race is one which their team wins, and the maximum number of eyeballs are directed to their logos.

For the riders, a good race may be one in which the hotels and transfers are favourable. I emailed Garmin-Sharp's David Millar to ask what he felt were the elements of a good bike race, and he listed 'good weather, a top-level peloton, interesting roads, definitive race-making terrain and crowds'. He also added 'history/prestige, which, although not imperative, adds a bit of magic'.

For the media, an overlapping combination of prestige, an already-famous winner or favourite who is from the same country, plus an accessible narrative – the story – make for a good race. A race organiser will have similar concerns, although they also want to showcase their region and terrain.

Fans have any number of different criteria they feel are important. More nationalistic cycling fans want one of their riders to win. Purists want exciting tactics, unpredictability or, paradoxically, predictability. You could, in short, argue that there are as many different opinions over what makes a good race as there are people in cycling.

But it's still possible to identify the various

elements that come into play when we dissect our sport. Fundamentally, bike racing remains a sport the point of which is to find out who wins the race – who harnessed strength, brains and luck better than his or her rivals – but it is also entertainment, and its popularity depends on how well it maintains the attention of its audience.

I've identified what I consider to be 13 basic elements I subconsciously use when I'm trying to make sense of a bike race. I will explain them here, though not necessarily in order of importance.

1 PLAYING FAIR

The foundation of sport is fairness and obeying the rules, and for a cycling race to have any sporting value whatsoever, it needs to have been raced clean. Cycling has suffered from over two decades following which fans have questioned whether any top-level races actually had sporting value. At the time, fans may have enjoyed Lance Armstrong, Marco Pantani, Jan Ullrich, Bjarne Riis et al winning the Tour de France, but these races were no more enjoyable as sporting spectacles as they would have been if they had been riding motorbikes instead.

The acid test, however, is the case of Alexandre Vinokourov. The Kazakh rider was frequently lauded for his attacking verve and exciting riding, although it was no great surprise when he tested positive in 2007. The question is, is it still exciting if a rider is only able to attack and ride away from the entire peloton because he has doped? The answer is, maybe so. But it's not sport.

2 UNPREDICTABILITY

Predicting what is going to happen in bike races takes up a huge amount of newsprint and bandwidth. I can't resist writing down who I think the top ten of the Tour de France is going to be, and who is going to win each of the Classics. I like thinking about the combination of previous results, momentum and current form, adding a bit of gut instinct and using that to predict the result of a race.

Sometimes it's easy – the last two Tours were so one-sided that the trophy engraver could have done his job half-way through the race and taken the rest of July off. Along with pretty much anybody with eyes, a brain and functioning critical faculties, I knew that Bradley Wiggins was going to win the 2012 yellow jersey, and that Chris Froome was going to win it in 2013.

But other times, I've predicted the winner in more difficult circumstances. I noticed in early 2011 that Nick Nuyens was riding especially well, winning the Dwars Door Vlaanderen after working Geraint Thomas over in the final kilometres. He'd had a couple of mediocre seasons, but, before that, had come second in the Tour of Flanders, and, a couple of years before again, had won Het Volk. I'd watched him at close hand during the 2005 Tour of Britain, which he won, and noticed that he'd said his biggest ambitions were the cobbled Classics. I had a hunch that the overwhelming favourite in Flanders, defending champion Fabian Cancellara, would be marked out of the race, and sensed that Nuyens had the tactical nous to take advantage. Add to that the fact Nuyens is Flandrian. It all pointed to him being a real dark horse in the event, which he indeed won.

However, I've got it wrong a lot more times than I've got it right when it comes to predicting races, and that is the point. We're not meant to know what is going to happen in a bike race, and I derive a huge amount of pleasure from being surprised by the result. I watched Milan-San Remo for over three hours in spring 2013, enjoying the gradual build-up of excitement as the race crossed the *capi*, Cipressa and Poggio. I remember the sudden realisation as the race hit the final 100 metres that Gerald Ciolek was going to win, after years of poor results, and riding for an obscure, wild-card team, and the moment of epiphany was far more enjoyable than if pre-race favourite Peter Sagan had duly sprinted to victory.

3 EXCITEMENT

Every year, at the Tour de France presentation in Paris, the organisers of the race, ASO, put on a montage showing highlights of the previous year's event. The footage is disproportionately weighted towards sprints and crashes, with a few mountain attacks for good measure.

It's easy to see why. These are the most televisually exciting moments of the race – dynamic, fast-moving and attention-grabbing. If you were trying to persuade your non-cycling-fan friend about the excitement of cycling, you might show them a video like this. But it's actually a bit of a lie – like a cricket Test match, a bike race can consist of long periods of relative inactivity, or at least slowly-building momentum, punctuated by moments of occasional drama.

Where is the excitement for the viewer who wants to watch the last two hours of a race? Bike racing is most exciting when it enters a period of flux. When attacks are going, or a sprint is unfolding, it takes a great deal of attention to actually follow the dynamics of the situation. The final 30 kilometres of the 2013 Amstel Gold Race, when enough small groups kept chipping off the front of the bunch that the balance of power invisibly tipped towards the escapees, was edge-of-the-seat stuff, as was Roman Kreuziger's exploit in just holding off a strong chase in the final two kilometres. Just when the race had seemed to fall into a routine of several years of straightforward group sprints up the finishing Cauberg climb, the race ripped up the formula.

Attacking riders are popular with the fans and the media, although they are rarely rewarded with victory, even though they are chiefly responsible for

enlivening the race. An example of the dispropor-
tionate way in which the spoils of victory are shared
between attackers and sprinters can be found in the
Danish rider Michael Mørkøv. In the 2012 Tour, he
was in the break of the day on the first three road
stages of the race, plus stage ten and 13. His total
reward, for around 1,000 kilometres of being off the
front of the bunch, was a few days in the polka-dot
jersey. It was ironic he got his biggest career win by
taking the sprint in the Vuelta's sixth stage this year,
after lone hero Tony Martin had been swallowed up
metres from the line following a long solo break.

But while for many fans aggressive riding is
what causes excitement, for others the sprints are as
compelling as the sport gets. The cliché is that the
sprinters are larger-than-life characters – egos in
Lycra – and their head-to-head battles are the most
exciting spectacles in bike racing. Ironically, most
sprint finishes are the product of formulaic racing –
the classic attack-hold-chase-catch template of most
flat Grand-Tour stages.

4 VARIETY

The 2012 Tour de France got a bad rap for being one
of the duller editions of the race. Bradley Wiggins
took a decisive lead early on, thanks to his strength in
the time trial, defensive riding in the mountains, and
an extraordinarily dominant team, and he kept his
boot on the throat of the race all the way to Paris.

But there was more to the race than the battle for the yellow jersey, even if that was the main subject of the mainstream media's coverage. The 2012 race was unusual in the number of stages that were contested by breakaways: of the nine road stages between stages eight and 17, the break was only successfully chased down in one. The tactical battles which unfolded between the riders in each of these breaks were far more entertaining than the general classification, and each was different. Thibaut Pinot came from behind on the Col de la Croix and won alone into Porrentruy, while his manager Marc Madiot screamed in delight from the team car. Thomas Voeckler won a desperate uphill sprint in Bellegarde. Luis Leon Sanchez outwitted Peter Sagan to win alone in Foix. Pierrick Fedrigo slowly dismantled the break into Pau, until there was only him and non-sprinter Christian Vande Velde left.

The best stage races are those which have multiple narratives and offer something out of the ordinary. That said, we may never get another Tour like 1992, when there was no stage won in a bunch sprint until stage ten, and then none again until the final stage in Paris. That year the GC battle was dull, too, with Miguel Indurain winning easily, but it gave the supporting cast a chance to shine.

5 SUSPENSE

It's amazing how often Grand Tours, at three weeks

in length, go down to the final few days. Logic dictates that, depending on the structure of the route, once a rider has proved himself the strongest, it's easier to defend a lead than it is for others to try to overturn it. But races don't always follow logic.

The 2012 Vuelta was essentially decided well into the last week, in unpredictable fashion, while the 2012 Giro was only won and lost on the last day's time trial. The most famous of them all, of course, is the 1989 Tour, when Greg LeMond took just enough time in the final day's time trial to beat Laurent Fignon by eight seconds.

Suspense is what keeps us hooked on both stage races and one-day events. Once I know who's going to win a race, my interest starts to tail off. The Tour de France organisers have designed most of their races since 2008 so that the really hard stages are backloaded into the final week, to guarantee that public interest is maintained. Sometimes it's backfired, such as in 2009, when the final showdown on Mont Ventoux turned into a tactically negative grind into a strong headwind, but as 2012 and 2013 have shown us, it's hard to maintain suspense when the winner looks invincible from the end of the first week onwards.

This is why Milan-San Remo, one of the flattest and most tactically straightforward races of the year, still manages to consistently be entertaining and exciting. The build-up of suspense and the fine balance of power between attackers and sprinters mean the race is often decided in the final few hundred metres.

6 AESTHETICS

If there was a more pleasing sight in professional cycling in 2013 than the Saxo Bank team having forced that winning echelon on stage 13 of the Tour, hammering away across the plains of France in the bright sunshine; or Marcel Kittel hurtling up the finishing straight in Paris; or Fabian Cancellara smoothly powering towards Oudenaarde along the N453 road in the Tour of Flanders; or Vincenzo Nibali emerging from the mist and snow to win at Tre Cime di Lavaredo, then I'd like to see it.

7 ENTERPRISE

Stage 13 of the 2013 Tour de France was by far the most tactically absorbing and spectacular day of the entire race. I'd grown so used to flat stages of the Tour offering little more than a slow-motion chase of an outgunned break, followed by a bunch sprint, that I'd have put my house on it happening again that day. Along with the Alpe d'Huez stage of the 2011 event, it was probably the best day's racing on the Tour de France in 25 years.

The carnage happened in waves. First, Omega Pharma, aided and abetted by Belkin, put Marcel Kittel out of the race early by hammering away into a moderate but persistent crosswind. Then Alejandro

Valverde got caught behind, and Belkin renewed their aggression. Finally, Saxo Bank engineered a final split, catching race leader Chris Froome cold, team time trialling away from virtually the entire field. The cherry on the cake was Mark Cavendish improvising a superb trap to ensnare Peter Sagan, his only real rival in the sprint, in the final kilometre.

Tactical racing is what separates cycling from more prosaic, logical sports like marathon running. The level of ability and preparation in the WorldTour these days is so high that tactical planning is essential in order to win races. Garmin-Sharp engineered a similar ambush in the second Pyrenean stage, to Bagneres de Bigorre, with Dan Martin winning the stage, and they applied a similar level of planning, on a larger scale, to supporting Ryder Hesjedal to a creative victory in the 2012 Giro d'Italia.

If cycling were logical, and the strongest rider won every time, it would get boring.

It's the tactics that makes the sport intriguing, whether it's the basic plan of putting a man in the break to help his team leader later on, the ability to force echelons in crosswinds, leading out a sprint or any one of hundreds of alternatives.

8 SCENERY

I couldn't help blurting out, when I encountered Christian Prudhomme about half-way through the 2013 Tour, that it had been the most beautiful edition

I can remember, in 29 years of following the race.
High Definition television, and well-planned helicop-
ter shots, help, but ASO made a deliberate decision
to make the 100th Tour a visually memorable one.

From the rugged, irregular topography of Corsica,
through arid Provence, to the idiosyncratic grandeur
of the Pyrenees, rural Brittany, Mont St Michel, the
charming emptiness of *La France Profonde*, Mont
Ventoux and the rocky, mighty Alps culminating in
a sparkling stage finish at Semnoz above the impossibly blue Lake Annecy, the 2013 Tour was a work of
art. It helped that the sun shone for almost the entire
duration, but by designing such a beautiful route, the
organisers made their own luck.

The Giro d'Italia is the Tour's equal for scenery
and the Vuelta a España has its moments. The Tour
of the Basque Country and Tour of Switzerland are
each held in outrageously beautiful landscapes, as
long as they are not obscured by rainclouds. Cycling
is a beautiful sport because it takes place in beautiful places. The scenery gives us something to look at
while we're waiting for the race to happen.

9 ATMOSPHERE

In the mid-2000s, I went to the Tour of Qatar a
couple of times. As a race, I quite like it, for the
simple fact that when the wind blows, there's no better demonstration of how echelons form.

But it might just as well have been held on the

Moon, there were so few spectators there.

The best races are given their atmosphere by the crowds by the side of the roads. The narrow, claustrophobic path riders beat through a tunnel of fans on a mountain road still brings me out in goose bumps (although I've got no time for the idiots who run alongside the riders – anybody who runs through a crowd while looking backwards deserves everything they get). The noise on the Muur van Geraardsbergen when the Tour of Flanders used the climb was like being at a football match.

Cycling belongs to the public. The people who support the riders and give races their atmosphere have made a deal: in return for not really knowing what is actually going on in the race until it reaches them, they are allowed to be close enough to the riders that they can hear their rasping breath on a mountain climb. The crowds are as much a part of the context of a bike race as the landscape it takes place in.

10 A GOOD WINNER

Fans differ over what makes a good winner of a race. Purists might think that as long as the winner earned his or her victory with either physical dominance or tactical astuteness, then it doesn't matter who it is. Others, like me, prefer an underdog to win, for the greater feeling of emotional engagement. Some like it when riders who are already big champions win races – again, the 1989 Tour was a classic in this respect, with three riders on the podium who had all previously won the yellow jersey. Some support a particular team or nationality. Cycling is less tribal than most other sports, but there are fans who don't mind who wins, as long as it's a rider from the team they support.

11 INTRIGUE

Professional cyclists are human beings, and they are as flawed as the rest of us. They are vulnerable to feelings of jealousy, ambition, greed and pride – and, in some cases, these emotions can be harnessed to motivate and fuel riders in a race. In others, they cause the same kind of political problems that they do in everyday life.

The 1986 Tour was, on the face of it, not the most exciting race. One team dominated, with La Vie Claire's Greg LeMond, Bernard Hinault and Andy Hampsten finishing first, second and fourth overall. Tactically, the team was able to crush the ambition out of all their rivals through sheer force of strength.

But the race was still a classic one, because of the soap-opera-level power struggle between five-time winner Hinault and champion-in-waiting LeMond. We were denied anything resembling a physical battle in 1986, but the psychological warfare was well worth it. And there have been numerous modern-day equivalents: the ill-concealed mutual

suspicion between Bradley Wiggins and Chris
Froome in the 2012 Tour, the scrabbling over team
leadership at BMC between Cadel Evans and Tejay
Van Garderen in the run-up to the 2013 Tour (there
was no winner in that battle) and the visible disman-
tling of Gilberto Simoni's team leadership by his
almost-unknown but stronger, younger team-mate
Damiano Cunego in the 2004 Giro.

Team Sky's PR operation did its best to cover
up the Wiggins-Froome rivalry in 2012, but they
didn't realise that during a tepid GC battle, it was the
most interesting story of the race. Fans like cycling
because it is emotionally engaging – just as the Greek
gods were all flawed in one way or another, our
cycling heroes are more accessible and interesting if
we see their human side.

12 BALANCE

The ideal bike race is one in which nobody can be
confident of winning. In a battle between the strongest rider, the most tactically astute rider, the most
aggressive rider and the rider with the most effective
team, the outcome is often not clear until it actually
happens. It's the balance between riders with different assets that makes cycling so compelling.

Even in a discipline like sprinting, where the pro-
tagonists have a similar primary weapon – finishing-
straight speed – each rider can bring a different set
of tactics and skills to the battle. At the Tour, Mark

Cavendish's pure speed was pitted against the effectiveness of André Greipel's lead-out, and the power and resilience of Marcel Kittel. It was Kittel who dominated this time, but both his main rivals will be back, with tweaks to their own tactics, and if Kittel shows up with the same game plan, it might not be enough again.

13 HISTORY

The more recent additions to the cycling calendar are finding that it takes more than a good PR campaign to establish themselves as real fixtures for the fans. Apart from the Strade Bianche race, which had its first edition in 2007, no modern race has captured the imagination in the same way the Grand Tours and the Classics do. The Tour Down Under, Tour of Qatar, Eneco Tour and even the Tour of Poland (which has a long history, but a relatively short one as a top-level professional race) are all still many years away from being thought of as equivalent to Paris-Nice, the Tour of Switzerland or the Tour of the Basque Country. It's safe to say that the Tour of Beijing will probably never reach that level.

It's no coincidence that, Strade Bianche aside, the biggest bike races are mostly around 90 or 100 years old. Races like the Vuelta and Paris-Nice are slightly younger, but have built up a level of support over decades of tradition. It's probably frustrating to the organisers of newer events that it's not possible to simply buy that level of loyalty or reputation from fans, but it's a lesson in the history of the sport.

Riders and fans have a keen sense of the history of cycling. When Mark Cavendish met André Darrigade, you could see the respect Cavendish had for a man who'd been his direct equivalent during the 1950s and 1960s.

These are the 13 elements I think decide how good a race has been. I've deliberately left out some, like *parcours*, because the most imaginative routes can sometimes be let down by formulaic racing, and the best racing sometimes happens on terrain where you'd expect it the least. And each cycling fan will give different weighting to each element.

But although I think all these elements are what make cycling exciting, it's not necessarily mandatory to quantify why some races are better than others, and some races are outright classics. If you enjoyed the race, that's enough.

Edward Pickering is a former deputy editor of *Cycle Sport* magazine, and has worked on every Tour de France since 2003. The best race ever, in his opinion, was the 1989 Tour, which scores highly on every single one of the 13 elements above, although he feels LeMond was a bit sneaky to use tri-bars. He is the author of *The Race Against Time*, and co-author, with Robbie McEwen, of *One Way Road*.

11

In homage to the game books
that were so popular in the 1980s,
in which the reader chooses his or
her own path through the story,
Ellis Bacon invites you to take
your place in the pro peloton.

This is a game for all wannabe
bike racers, aged eight to 80, in
which *you* make all the decisions.

YOU ARE THE PRO

BY ELLIS BACON

It's the start of the 2013 season, and you've joined one of Europe's biggest professional teams, making the step up from a smaller pro outfit where you'd spent a number of years.

You've only got a one-year contract, however, which means that you need to impress – and fast.

You've been assured that you'll be riding your first Grand Tour this season: that is, either the Giro d'Italia, the Tour de France or the Vuelta a España. It was part of the reason you chose to sign on the dotted line. That and the fact that you're not getting any younger, and were fearing that the chance to test yourself at the highest level was in danger of slipping away.

Early on, the management tell you that you're on the shortlist for the Vuelta – the Tour of Spain – in late August. The Giro and the Tour will have to remain on your wish list for at least another year.

After kicking your season off with the Tour of the Mediterranean, in the south of France, in February, the manager then offers you the choice of riding either Paris-Nice or Tirreno-Adriatico as your first top-level WorldTour race.

Paris-Nice – 'The Race to the Sun' – is a week of racing that has it all: a short prologue time trial, sprints, climbs, and a mountain time trial up to the top of the Col d'Éze, overlooking Nice, to finish things off.

Tirreno-Adriatico is a week-long stage race that takes riders across the width of Italy's 'calf', from the Tyrrhenian Sea to the Adriatic Sea. Like Paris-Nice, 'The Race of the Two Seas' features plenty of climbing, but it's nevertheless geared slightly more towards sprinters, plus there's also a team time trial.

Which iconic week-long stage race are you going to choose?

Now it's decision time...
■ Do you choose to ride Paris-Nice?
If so, go to page 207
■ Or, to choose to race Tirreno-Adriatico,
turn to page 209

You decide that you'd prefer to go to Paris-Nice.
You love France, and you speak the language, and,
having already raced at the Tour of the Med, you're
happy for your French adventure to continue.

Plus you've always wanted to ride this illustrious
event: a mini Tour de France, which, like its older
sibling, combines sprints, climbs and time trials into
one always-exciting week of racing.

Things start well when you creep into the top
20 in the short, three-kilometre prologue time trial
around Houilles, just outside Paris.

You're the best-placed rider on the team, which
means that everyone works for you on the opening
road stage the next day.

A three-man break gets away almost from the
gun, but they're reeled in again with just over 20
kilometres to go, and it looks as though it's going to
be a bunch sprint.

However, a number of small crashes in the final
20 kilometres causes a split in the bunch, and you
find yourself on the wrong side of it, losing almost
two minutes by the finish in Nemours.

Your moment in the limelight is over, and you put
yourself to work for your team-mates for the rest of
the week, fetching food and water bottles for them
from the team car, and sheltering your team leader
from the wind.

In the final time trial, you've got nothing left,
and finish well off the pace. But you've ridden better

than your team had expected and, due to your good form – and, you later discover, your team leader's insistence – you're offered the opportunity to ride the illustrious Milan-San Remo one-day Classic in north-west Italy the following week.

You don't have to think about it for a second; of course you'll ride it. It's the kind of race you've dreamed about doing and, having just ridden Paris-Nice, you'll be able to tick off two of the most famous races in the world before March is over.

However, after just a couple of days at home, you receive a call telling you that, due to a team-mate's injury, your race schedule might need to be changed again so that you ride the Giro d'Italia in May, swapping with the rider in question so that he'll instead ride the Vuelta in your place later in the season.

You can't believe your luck – a chance to ride the Giro! – but the kicker is that it would mean missing Milan-San Remo after all, and that you'd instead rest before preparing for the mountains of the Giro with some shorter stage races.

So, where would you prefer to go?

Now it's decision time...
■ To try your luck on the famous roads of Milan-San Remo, **turn to page 212**
■ To rest up ahead of riding the iconic Giro d'Italia, **turn to page 215**

You opt for Tirreno-Adriatico, and arrive in San Vincenzo, on Italy's west coast, excited to be riding such an iconic race. The opening 17-kilometre team time trial is the sort of event that you've been brought onto the team for, thanks to your ability against the clock, and the team's thrilled when you play your part in helping your eight-man squad to blast home to fourth place on the first stage, just 17 seconds shy of the winning team, who are also the reigning world champions in the discipline.

The wet weather that blights the opening few days eventually subsides during the fourth stage between Narni and the summit finish at Prati di Tivo, and so you look for your team-mates in order to take their rain jackets back to the team car in the convoy of cars following the race.

You collect all the jackets together by stuffing them up the back and front of your jersey, and tell your team-mates that you'll be back with some fresh water bottles.

You stop pedalling and enjoy the feeling of drifting back through the other 175 riders that make up the peloton, and then keep your wits that bit more about you as you meet the following team cars.

Your team's car is about eighth in line, and, as the *directeur sportif* pulls alongside you and buzzes open the car window, you start pulling out the jackets and hand them to him, holding onto them for just a few seconds longer than is strictly necessary to take advantage of getting pulled along by the car on the now steepening road. It's the old 'sticky bottle' trick, so called because the same ruse is often used when collecting bottles from the car: holding on a little longer to a bottle to get a bit of a pull and save some energy.

The last jacket doesn't come free from the back of your jersey quite as easily as the others did, but, when it does, one of the arms flails behind it, dropping down dangerously close to your back wheel.

You go to quickly pull it up and out of the way, but the whole jacket is pulled from your grip, and your bike rears up in front of you as the back wheel locks completely, and you have a split second to realise that the rogue sleeve has indeed got caught up in the spokes – and that this isn't going to end well.

You're flipped into the air, and then land, hard, on top of your bike. For a moment, everything's quiet as the peloton, in the distance, nudges further away from you, the race continuing, and the team cars drive on by, including your own, not being able to just stop on a sixpence.

Then the pain comes: a building, throbbing pain all the way around your thigh and hip. You've crashed numerous times before, and have broken your collarbone twice, but this is something new. Your leg locks up, and, as you lie back on the road, the back of your helmet touching the road, pulling your glasses up and off your face, you know that you're not about to get up and carry on. Spectators chitter and chatter around you in Italian, and two men lift your bike up from beneath you, readying it, willing you to get back on and back into the race.

You feel sick with the pain, and soon the race doctor is alongside you.

'Pelvis, pelvis,' she says to your *directeur sportif* when he appears, having pulled over and run back down the road. He puts his hand on your shoulder, and tells you that your race is over.

An ambulance takes you to the local hospital, where an X-ray reveals multiple fractures to your pelvis. You're instructed to rest for at least three weeks, and to then only start training again on your home trainer, 'with a cushion on the saddle if need be', the doctor grins, a little too joyously for your liking.

After around eight weeks, during which time you're able to get back to training on the road, and after another hospital check-up, you're reassessed by the team doctor, who tells you that you're close to being back to a level of fitness similar to where you were before the crash.

You realise that you've been relatively lucky – that you could have been off the bike for a lot longer – and your team tells you to keep training and to be ready for the start of the Vuelta in late August.

Turn to page 218

You roll out of Milan's Piazza Castello for the start of Milan-San Remo, and settle in for 298 kilometres in the saddle – the longest one-day race on the pro calendar.

With around a quarter of the distance covered, you get that unmistakeable feeling that you're on a good day, despite the freezing temperatures.

But the weather gets worse, and blizzards force the race organisers to shorten the route. Back in the warmth of your team bus, you're ferried more than 50 kilometres further on, over the climbs of the Turchino and Le Manie.

Nicely warmed up – literally – you restart the race feeling even more ready for the job in hand, and you're still with the somewhat depleted peloton when it climbs over the Cipressa. You're even still there on the final climb of the Poggio, where your team leader orders you and your few remaining team-mates to the front to help reel in a small group that got away on the climb.

At the top of the Poggio, you take the famously bumpy left-hand turn onto the start of the descent into San Remo. You can see the three breakaway riders, only around 20 seconds ahead, and, as what's left of the bunch stretches out into a snaking single line of riders, you grit your teeth, and try your best to keep your hands off the brakes.

Which would have been fine if your team-mate in front of you hadn't hopelessly misjudged one of the

sweeping bends. While he topples over one of the
roadside barriers – rather elegantly, you think – you
slam on your brakes, causing your bike to slide away
from beneath you.

You hit your knee hard on the ground, and then
slide along behind your bike before finally coming to
quite a gentle halt alongside the barrier a little further
down the descent from your team-mate.

The rest of the peloton swoosh by, missing you
by inches, and a spectator appears next to you with
your bike. You go to get up, but that's when you feel
it: there's a gaping wound on your knee, like some
hideous mouth, thick with bright-red blood. You
gasp with pain as you jump on your bike to begin
your pursuit of the race, but, when you start pedalling again, the pain of the opening-closing, opening-
closing wound forces you to freewheel for the rest
of the descent.

Your race is over, and, as you pedal the remaining
painful kilometres to the finish by standing out of
the saddle to stretch your knee as little as possible,
you worry whether your season might be over, too.

At the finish, you head straight to the team bus,
and look down at your leg again. Most of your lower
leg is crusted in blood.

A race ambulance takes you to the local hospital,
where your wound is cleaned and stitched up. X-rays
show no real damage, but the deep cut is going to
take some time to heal.

Once you're back home, your managers email through a revised race schedule, with your next race due to be the Tour de Wallonie, in Belgium, at the end of July.

You're disappointed to see that the Vuelta has been removed from your new programme.

'We're sorry, but we just don't think you're going to have enough racing in your legs by then once you've recovered from your injury,' one of the *directeurs sportifs* tells you over the phone.

So there'll be no three-week Grand Tour for you this season after all, and, if you can't get a contract extension, you might have to accept that you'll never get your chance to ride a Grand Tour at all.

You head to Belgium in late July in a determined mood.

Turn to page 227

A beautiful hot, sunny day in Naples welcomes you and the other 206 starters of the 96th edition of the Giro d'Italia.

The opening stage has 'bunch sprint' written all over it, and your team's sprinter is champing at the bit for a chance to win the stage and take the race's first pink leader's jersey, even though he's been warned by the team manager that he shouldn't expect any kind of lead-out train as the squad will be saving itself for the team time trial the following day, and that he'll get help in the sprints later in the race.

Your bit has already been thoroughly champed as a result of the nerves you experience in the lead-up to such a big race, but, although it's a huge deal, the enthusiastic and happy Italian spectators soon make you feel like a rockstar, and it's not long before you're posing for pictures with fans and signing autographs with the best of them, even though you're pretty certain they don't know who you are.

'You're a Giro rider now,' one of your more experienced team-mates points out, as if you need reminding, but you resolve there and then to try to enjoy the experience, as much as a three-week race can possibly be enjoyed.

There's nevertheless a strained atmosphere during the team meeting on the bus ahead of stage one when the team management reminds you all – and your sprinter in particular – to try to keep your powder dry for the following day's team time trial where it's thought you have a real chance of taking the stage victory if everything goes right.

The first 100 kilometres of the first stage is uneventful enough, with a seven-man break going clear almost from the gun, which the sprinters' teams never allow to get a lead of more than a couple of minutes, and they're caught with around 40 kilometres left to race.

You fight hard to stay as close as possible to the front and out of danger of any crashes, and, with around 30 kilometres to go, that all-too-familiar sound of brakes squealing, men swearing and people hitting the deck reaches your ears – from behind you.

Looking back, you can't believe what you see: a huge pile-up, with only the 35 or so of you nearest the front unaffected.

A couple of the sprinters' teams have an almost full complement of riders in the front group, who push on while the rest of you dither, trying to decide whether to keep racing or wait for your team-mates.

Just then, your team sprinter – having avoided the crash – all but clips you around the helmet, ordering you to ride and to try to get him the stage victory. With the stage winner also set to get the leader's jersey, he clearly fancies his chances from a smaller group.

That's when the screaming in your ear starts: it's your *directeur sportif* from back in the team car telling everyone to wait. Your sprinter theatrically flicks his radio earpiece out of his ear. 'RIDE!' he screams at you.

You're caught in two minds. What are you going to do?

It's decision time...
■ To stay with the front group to try to help your team-mate win the stage, **turn to page 220**
■ To obey team orders and wait for your other team-mates who have been involved in the crash, **turn to page 223**

The Vuelta kicks off in the Galician town of
Vilanova de Arousa with a 27.4-kilometre team time
trial, finishing further south in Sanxenxo – a flat, but
potentially windy, course on Spain's Atlantic coast.

It feels to you as though the season is almost over,
despite it still only being late August. Plus, because
of your injury, you've missed out on spending much
time with your team-mates, and have had to watch
the best of them take on the Tour de France on
television while you trained at home, usually alone.

You wonder how well you'll gel with them for
the opening stage of the Vuelta. It's your chance to
impress them – to impress everyone – and yet you
feel like a stranger who doesn't really deserve to be
there. In the days leading up to the start of the race,
you have to keep reminding yourself that this is the
Vuelta: your first Grand Tour – and possibly your
last, if you don't pull yourself together.

With three weeks of racing ahead of you, it's
incredibly daunting – week-long stage races are the
longest events you've ever done before – but you've
trained hard and recovered well from your accident,
so there's nothing for it but to put your head down
and give it everything you've got.

Out on the team time trial warm-up you all do
together, something seems to click. These boys seem
to know exactly what to do, and you, as somewhat
of a time-trial specialist, can either benefit from their
experience or allow them to overshadow you.

Fifteen kilometres into the stage, the speed and power you're producing as a team is phenomenal. A couple of kilometres later, you realise that you're struggling to hold the team-mate in front's wheel. You shout out for them to knock the pace off slightly, which they do for about a kilometre – you'd all been told to call out if you needed to; it was felt that a complete nine-man team staying together would have the best chance of victory – but another kilometre or so further on, you realise that you may have to drop off the pace, which wouldn't be the end of the world, you decide, as each team only gets timed on the fifth man across the line anyway.

Now it's decision time...
■ To drop off the pace and try to save yourself for the three weeks of racing still to come, **turn to page 245**
■ To absolutely bury yourself to stay in contact to try to help the team to the win, **turn to page 229**

It's a numbers game now, you decide, and with the front group reduced to around 30 riders after some of the riders unaffected by the crash choose to wait for their team-mates, the race is on.

You feel bad disobeying team orders, but if you can help your sprinter win the stage, it'll be well worth it, and you bury yourself to stay with the front group, which does stay away, and are surprised to be able to give him a pretty decent lead-out in the final kilometre, despite all the other sprinters' teams trying to take control. For a moment you think you might have done enough as your man hits the front of the race in first place with 400 metres to go.

But he's swamped by the other, better sprinters, in the group, and ends up eighth.

He thanks you on the other side of the finish line, and tells you that you did the right thing – that the two of you tried.

Team management don't see it that way, however, and while you escape a major dressing down, your sprinter feels the full force of the manager's loud and sweaty reaction – not to mention his less than salubrious breath – at the hotel that night.

Your team-mates have all lost over two minutes, which means the plan to try to put one of them in the leader's jersey has fallen by the wayside. Your sprinter reminds the manager that both he and you still have a chance having finished in the front group, but it seems to fall on deaf ears.

The next day, in the team time trial, held over just 17.4 kilometres, your sprinter drops off the very high pace early on – he's no time triallist – which leaves you in the unreal position of possibly taking the leader's jersey if your team can win the stage. But that will only happen if you can keep pace with your team-mates, and, after a 30-kilometre all-out effort the day before, you struggle to stay in touch.

The team has the dilemma of choosing whether to try to nurse you home on the off-chance that you can still take the jersey, or press on without you to try to win the stage and get back some of the time lost to the crash on the first stage. They choose the former, and you're left red-faced in more ways than one when the team comes home in only tenth place. There'll be no leader's jersey for you today.

Your manager comes to your hotel room later that evening and tells you not to worry too much about it, reminding you that things rarely go to plan in bike racing.

You struggle through the rest of the Giro, helping your team-mates as much as you can, and following the management's instructions to the letter.

Sheer bloody-mindedness gets you to Milan, and your team is pleased with the work you've done.

The Tour de France is of course not on your schedule, and instead you're told that your next race will be the Tour de Wallonie, in Belgium, at the end of July, which gives you plenty of time to rest after the Giro, and you take advantage of your downtime to visit your family and friends back home before resuming your training schedule in mid-June.

___

Turn to page 227

___

You tell your sprinter that you're going to wait for your team-mates, as instructed by your *directeur sportif*, and wish him luck as he shakes his head and tags on to the back of the front group who will likely fight it out between them for the stage win.

Sure enough, it's quite some time before all your team-mates are back on their bikes again, but luckily none of them are seriously injured, and you join a huge group of riders who work together in an effort to limit the time they'll lose to the front group, trying to catch them, ideally.

In the end, you close to within a minute of the lead group, and discover after you've crossed the line that your team's sprinter finished tenth on the stage.

He doesn't want to talk to you, feeling betrayed that you didn't try to help him, but your team-mates and the team management tell you that you made the right decision, and attention soon turns to the tactics to employ for the next day's team time trial.

You're expected to play a key role, and to try to stay with the team for as long as possible, even though the clock will stop on the fifth man out of nine, so losing riders along the way isn't the end of the world.

However, with your sprinter on the same time as the race leader, and with a real chance of your team taking the stage victory, you're under strict instructions to try to shepherd your sprinter home without leaving him behind.

Out on the road, you're like a well-oiled machine, and you manage not to lose a single rider along the 17.4-kilometre course. It's enough to give the team the lead on the stage, and you have a tense wait to see whether any of the teams starting behind you can beat you.

They can't, and your team wins the stage, which none of you can believe. It gives your sprinter the pink leader's jersey, too, and he makes a point of giving you a big hug on the podium – both of you drenched in Prosecco – and apologises for the day before.

You're thrilled – for him, for you, and for the whole team. This is what all the years of effort have been for: a chance to stand on the podium as one of the best bike racers in the world.

And although your team loses the leader's jersey the next day, the Giro stage win gives you the confidence you so badly needed to get through the rest of the race, and you busy yourself with helping your team-mates in whatever way you can, with no personal ambitions other than to get to Milan.

At one point along the way, one of the team's big stars even talks about you being selected for the Tour, but your *directeurs sportifs* assure you that that isn't going to happen.

Your full-on season so far, off the back of a big winter of training, encourages the management to allow you a long break until your next race, which will be the Tour of Poland at the end of July.

You even get to enjoy watching the Tour de France on television, which you and your flat-mate agree seems extremely decadent, but you make sure to get your training done earlier in the day, allowing for a guilt-free couple of hours of TV-watching on the sofa once you're back.

You head to the Tour of Poland with a decent team, which includes a team-mate who managed to win a stage at the Tour de France. He is treated, and acts like, an absolute hero, and it's hoped his form can net him a high overall finish in Krakow – Poland's 'second city'.

Your job is to look after his every need, while keeping one eye on giving the individual time trial on the final stage a good go yourself.

By the time the final stage comes around, your team-mate still has a real chance of winning overall, sitting in third place, just a few seconds off the lead.

But it's now out of your hands; it's up to him to produce a good time trial, and you set about trying to do the same.

It's only over 37 kilometres, but with a hilly first half and a gently downhill second and final sector. Your team-mates who have already finished their runs all have differing opinions about how best to approach it.

In the start house, before haring down the ramp to get your time trial underway, you need to make up your mind about how to gauge your effort so as to achieve the fastest possible time.

Now it's decision time...
■ To stamp over the climbs, giving it everything you have, and then just try to hold on as best you can for the second half of the course, **turn to page 234**
■ To ride a more measured race, staying within yourself on the climbs before unleashing everything on the second half of the course to the finish, **turn to page 235**

On a hot opening day of the Tour de Wallonie,
word comes through that one of the team's riders
has won a stage of the Tour de France. That means
champagne at dinner for you, and, as you toast your
team-mate's success in France, you get a flush of
team-building spirit with your own team-mates here
in Belgium, and feel certain that you want to stay
with them for the following season – should you be
offered a contract extension.

A top domestic team back in your home country
has already been in touch to tentatively see what your
plans are, and to potentially offer you leadership of
their squad, although the transfer 'window' doesn't
officially open until August 1st.

It's been a baptism of fire so far here at the highest level, but you've told your friends and family –
and yourself – that you'd like a longer crack at trying
to move up rather than taking a 'step down' back to
a team closer to home.

The second day of the Tour de Wallonie is
brutal, with the wind having picked up compared
to the previous day. Only two of your team-mates
finish in the front group, and the squad's highest-
placed rider is down in 48th place, almost two
minutes off the leader.

The team manager joins the *directeur sportif* in the
hotel's meeting room after dinner that night to talk
tactics with you, urging you all that they need to see
some better results for the sponsors.

The next day, the DS stands up in the team bus just before the start of the third stage to remind you all of what was said at the hotel last night, and to say that the team's main sponsors are in fact visiting the race today.

'I'm just asking you all to do your best,' he says, but you can tell that it's a veiled threat. The team really needs to perform, else tonight's pep talk isn't going to be quite as friendly...

It's a quiet roll-out at the start, and, when the flag drops for the official start, not one rider tries their luck. The peloton is in a relaxed mood.

You move towards the front with a few of your team-mates. Your team leader chats to the race leader – they're former team-mates – who says that they'll be trying to keep the race together, and that they'd appreciate any help in return for helping your team set up a bunch sprint. You team leader laughs that you've been told to be a bit more active than that, and, just then, your attention is grabbed by a flash of colour. It's not a race vehicle, or the crowd flashing by. Two riders have attacked, and with the team management's appeal for a bit more effort on your team's part playing on your mind, you have to make a quick decision...

- To go with the attack, **turn to page 230**
- To stay put in the peloton for now, **turn to page 232**

You give yourself the swiftest of pep talks, remembering what you're here to do and – with the chance to win a stage of one of the biggest races in the world – you tell your legs to shut up and push on. You cross the finish line in Sanxenxo absolutely spent, and one of your team-mates has to almost catch you as you threaten to topple sideways off your bike. Your team has set the best time, and no one is able to beat it.

You're a Grand Tour stage winner, and, up on the podium, as the Cava corks pop, you and your team-mates bask in the glory of a job well done.

You work hard for the team in the weeks that follow. On the second rest day, the national federation coach calls to say you've been selected for both the time trial and the road race at the world championships in Florence, Italy, in September.

If you can complete the Vuelta, you'll arrive in Florence in the form of your life, but during a tough, cold and wet final week, you pick up a chest infection, and your team doctor agrees that it's probably best that you head home to recover ahead of the Worlds. 'There'll be other opportunities to complete a Grand Tour,' your team manager tells you by way of consolation before you leave for home. His smile suggests that the team might want to extend your contract, and he says they'll be in touch soon.

Turn to page 237

Instinctively, you react to the attack, and sprint onto the second rider's back wheel. One of your team-mates gives you a shout of encouragement, and the conversation you were a part of just a few seconds before fades behind you.

Finally. This is what you came here for. Your two breakaway companions are not big names – a Belgian from a Belgian team and a Frenchman from one of the other Belgian squads. Like you, they're early in their careers, out to impress – quite possibly chasing a new contract, like you.

At 168.5 kilometres, between Beaufays and Bastogne, it's the shortest stage of the five-day race, but one of the hilliest, too, and you've left the protection of the bunch early. You take a look back, and the peloton's still spread out across the road, with no sign of anyone wanting – or needing – to chase you. Yet.

The next ten minutes go by in a flash of effort, turn-taking at the front and encouragement from your respective team cars who have slotted in behind you, between you and the bunch. Once you've established a four-minute lead, your DS tells you to try to measure your effort – that you've got a long day ahead of you.

At the feed zone, you grab your lunch, and, a few minutes later, having thrown away what you don't want to eat – damn marmalade sandwiches again, which you hate, and are beginning to wonder whether your team *soigneurs* are playing some kind of joke on you, as they're always laughing about how that's what English-speaking riders are supposed to eat – you're told that a huge crash has taken down a number of the favourites, and that in the resulting chaos your lead has gone up to well over five minutes.

The three of you decide to push on a lot harder, sharing the work well, and, with 20 kilometres to go, your lead is still three-and-a-half minutes.

You look at the other riders. The Frenchman you know from your junior days; he's a fast sprinter, and took the silver medal at the under-23 world championships one year. You know little of the Belgian, but he doesn't look like much of a sprinter.

You know that the best course of action in order to maintain your time advantage is to stay together. However, if you come to the line with the French rider, you know second – or perhaps only third if the Belgian does turn out to be quite handy – is the best result you can hope for. If the bunch doesn't catch you first, that is.

It could be now or never… But is it still too early to try to go it alone?

It's decision time…
■ To keep working together with your breakaway companions, **turn to page 238**
■ To put in an attack to try to drop the other two riders, **turn to page 242**

You decide to stay put, ready in case there is a counter-move. But it never comes. The race leader's team controls the pace, never letting the breakaway gain more than five minutes, and, with 40 kilometres to go, two of the sprinters' teams go to the front.

Although your squad doesn't have any particularly fast men here at the race – the team's stars have been in France at the Tour – your team leader nevertheless decides to put you and a couple of your team-mates on the front to help the other teams out and ensure that the break is reeled in.

With just over five kilometres to go, it's all over for the break of two, and a determined hush falls over the peloton as it gears up for a bunch sprint. Tired from helping out, you drift backwards, rolling in at the back of the main bunch.

Back at the team hotel, you and your team-mates get the ear-bashing you've been expecting, and, quite frankly, probably deserve.

The rest of the week flashes by in a blur of travelling, eating, sleeping, massage and racing – the latter rather lacklustre from both you and your team-mates. After the race, you head home to your empty apartment, get back to training, and await your schedule for the rest of the season's races.

After two weeks, you fire off an email to team management, jokingly asking if they've forgotten about you. There's no reply. After waiting a few more days, you call one of the *directeurs sportifs*, who tells you that they're struggling to work out some of the riders' schedules, but that they'll be in touch again soon.

In the meantime, you continue to train hard, whilst becoming increasingly nervous. You call one of your team-mates from the Tour de Wallonie – a fellow 'first year' with the team – which at least reassures you, as he's not heard anything, either.

Eventually, an email pops into your inbox telling you to be ready for the upcoming World Ports Classic. You're back on, but are concerned about the team's apparent lack of interest in you – and in particular about the lack of any real structured race programme going forward.

Turn to page 247

You decide to push hard on the climbs right from the start. There are three climbs in total, and although none of them could exactly be classed as mountains, the first and third are both a couple of kilometres long, while the second one, while not as steep, goes on for about five kilometres.

Already on the second climb, you realise that you've made a grave mistake in going out so hard, and the last 15 kilometres almost tip you over the edge. From the fast downhill off the final climb, the road gradually evens out by the finish, but you cross the line in a state of exhaustion. You think you hear your *soigneur* tell you that you're nevertheless in second place, but it's some minutes before you're in any fit state to try to get it confirmed.

By the time you've recovered enough to check the standings, the better riders have come home, bumping you down to 11th place, which still isn't a bad result. Your team-mate managed to finish second on the stage, which also moved him up a place to second overall, and you head home as part of a happy team.

A few days later, you get the call that you'd been hoping for, if not expecting: you've been selected for the world championships in Florence, Italy, by your national team, and will be riding both the time trial and the road race.

Turn to page 237

You decide that a more measured approach would be more sensible, and, although you hurt yourself on the climbs, you make sure that you've got something in the tank for the second half of the course.

You fly off the final climb, diving down the descent at what you later see on your power meter was over 90kph.

Approaching the finish, you push hard all the way to the line, glancing up at the clock only once you're safely over the line.

For a moment, you think that what you see must be some kind of mistake: you're in first place. There are still some very decent time-triallists to come – the world's very best, in fact – but in the meantime you're ushered to the 'hot seat', close to the podium, where a TV camera remains permanently trained on you as the current leader of the stage, capturing your expression as riders try, but fail, to knock you off your perch.

With only two riders left to finish, you realise that the worst you can finish is third, which would be an extraordinary result. Sure enough, the penultimate rider knocks you off the top of the leaderboard, and before he can even 'steal' your seat, the last rider comes home, beating you both.

Clearly your TV-watching 'training' has paid dividends! You've been beaten here in Poland only by the current Olympic champion and the world champion. It's a huge result for you and the team, and your national federation calls you at the hotel that night to tell you that you've been selected to ride both the time trial and the road race at the world championships in Florence, Italy, in September.

You're thrilled, and knuckle down to training – mainly on your time-trial bike – in the hope of repeating your Polish time-trial success and winning a medal at the Worlds.

Turn to page 244

In Florence at the world championships, you train hard on the 58-kilometre-long time trial course, and, when race day comes, you're feeling confident that your really-rather-decent first season at the top level will stand you in good stead.

Apart from a short climb in the first ten kilometres, it's an otherwise flat, fast course, which suits you down to the ground. You're one of the relatively later starters, and you blast across the finish line in sixth place, although you know that there are going to be a few more decent riders to finish who are likely to beat your time.

Nevertheless, you're astonished when only three more riders beat you, meaning that you're the ninth best – top ten! – time trial rider in the world.

A couple of days later, on the day before the road race, you and your agent join your team manager for lunch, where he produces a one-year contract extension for you to sign. He tells you that they're pleased with your progression, and apologises that it isn't a two-year one, but you're ecstatic nevertheless.

The road race goes well enough, and, although you don't finish the race, you're thrilled to be able to play your part in helping your compatriot to a bronze medal.

But you're already thinking about the following season, and your new contract means that you now you have the chance to do it all over again…

Congratulations – you earned a new contract!

'On travaille ensemble, okay?' you say to the other two, and you assume they understand your suggestion to keep things as they are and hope to stay away from the chasers behind to the end.

Top three in a stage of the Tour de Wallonie would be a massive result in your first year with a top European cycling team, you decide.

The encouragement from your DS in the team car seems to say as much, at least. 'You can do this!' he shouts at you from the open window of the car. He hands you an energy gel, and you eat it imme-diately, realising that you've forgotten to eat much lately in the excitement of the moment.

'Come on – you can do this!' he shouts again, and whether he actually means hold the chasers off all the way to the finish or that you can win the stage, you're not sure.

With around a kilometre and a half to go, the Belgian puts in a dig, flying off the front. The French-man covers the move easily, and you have no prob-lem following his wheel. Approaching the red 'kite' suspended above the road, signifying a kilometre to go, the Belgian tries again, and again it's the French-man, and not you, who closes the gap. A clue! The Belgian knows he can't win in a sprint. You know you can't, either, but the Belgian is now shattered from his efforts. He's played his last card.

'Second!' you dare to think to yourself, and allow yourself a small smile, which anyone watching would assume was a grimace. The French rider's got the bit between his teeth, and doesn't slow down once the Belgian's caught again. You pass the Belgian and, when you look back, he's already two bike lengths behind you.

You look past the French rider in front, and see there's an almost 90-degree bend with 600 metres to go. He's pushing on, confident of just riding you off his wheel in the final sprint, and you resolve to stay as close behind him as you can, to save face, if nothing else.

He barrels into the corner, far faster than you thought he would, and now it's you leaving a small gap.

But it's lucky you did: he's gone too fast, and slams into the crowd barrier on the outside of the corner. The win is yours for the taking.

In the photo of the finish – which will later hang for years in your hallway – there's you giving as traditional a two-handed salute as you can muster while two distressed-looking riders, one each side of the road, either side of you, around ten bike lengths in arrears, roll home. The Frenchman got third in the end…

On the finish line, everything erupts. You suddenly don't know what nationality you are. Are you Belgian now? The excitement of everyone is frenetic. Microphones and voice recorders are thrust in front of you – perhaps only four or five of them, but suddenly you feel very small, slumped over the front of your bike. The questions are in a mixture of Dutch and French, but then one in English makes you lift your head.

'I can't believe it,' you hear yourself say. 'I thought I might get third. Second was the best I was hoping for. This is the greatest win of my career.'

You sound like someone else – like other riders you've seen on TV. You always imagined you'd say something clever, witty, but nothing's in your control at this moment.

Your *soigneur* – the one who makes you the marmalade sandwiches – puts a towel over your shoulders, and leads you through the hubbub to a small tent, where he washes your face with one of those towelling mittens you've seen winners on the receiving end of, and gives you a fresh, long-sleeved jersey to put on.

On the podium you squint into the bright, evening sun and milk the applause, throwing your winner's bouquet into the crowd with no one to give it to otherwise. It's a feeling you haven't had for a very long time – that of a winner.

In the weeks that follow the stage win, you feel as though you've cracked it. You're one of the boys; the *directeurs sportifs* speak to you much more readily, and even ask your opinion when it comes to tactics at some of the races that follow.

Your schedule for the rest of the season is drawn

up, and includes the GP Ouest-France – a one-day race based around the small Breton town of Plouay – followed by a trip to Canada to ride the two new WorldTour one-day races in Quebec and Montreal.

They all go well, but you return home feeling as though you haven't actually shone as either an indispensable help to the team, or really demonstrated the makings of a future star, despite your somewhat lucky stage win at the Tour de Wallonie.

You're soon cheered up again, however, after taking a call from your national federation, offering you the chance to end your season with the world championships, riding for your national team in the time trial and the road race. It was at the world championships last year that you signed your one-year contract with the team, and so you're hoping that history might repeat itself.

Turn to page 244

You know it's a big risk, but you decide that if you don't try anything, the chance of a stage win is going to pass you by.

There's a small rise ahead, and, after your turn at the front – during which you try to soft-pedal a little – you allow yourself to drift to the back of the group. It's the French rider's turn on the front, and, as he hits the small climb, you go for it, trying to make it the strongest, fastest, smoothest attack of your life. You actually hear the French rider grunt as he tries to react, and in your peripheral vision you can see you've got a bit of a gap.

But where's the Belgian? For a split second, you think he's gone – that you've dropped him – but then you realise that he's fairly easily followed you; that he's right there on your back wheel.

You curse him in your head, quickly and efficiently, as this is no time for thinking. It's as long as it takes for him to somehow counter-attack, and this time you've got nothing left as he disappears up the road.

You push on, helped by the French rider, who's fought his way back up to you, but you can't catch the Belgian rider, and the Frenchman beats you easily in the sprint for second.

But third on a stage of the Tour de Wallonie, staying away from the bunch… You're still delighted. Your *soigneur* greets you with a towel, a can of drink, and some encouraging words. You have to be pleased with that, he tells you, and you are.

Later, at the hotel – and despite the congratulations and 'hard lucks' from everyone on the team bus – your team managers actually seem quite disappointed that you couldn't convert your one-in-three chance into victory. They tell you they're experiencing real pressure from the sponsors to win more races, and urge you to try again as soon as you can.

You head to bed with a mix of emotions, and wonder what you can do to improve further.

You spend the rest of the race working for your team-mates and, at this point of the season, wonder whether you'll get another chance to show your worth again.

Turn to page 247

At the time-trial world championships in Florence, you're able to put your fine form to good use against the best in the world, and are over the moon to finish fourth, just off the pace of the medallists, two of whom are past winners.

The road race, three days later, is a race too far, though, and you pull out around the half-way mark having done what you can for your national team on what is a very hilly, tough circuit.

Despite the occasional setback, you have to admit that your season couldn't really have gone much better – and what a way to end it at the Worlds!

Almost a year to the day after you'd been offered a one-year contract, your team manager finds you after the road race to offer you a two-year contract with the team, determined that your time-trialling ability can help the squad to win team time trials in the Grand Tours, while promising that you'll be given the opportunity to target stage wins in week-long stage races, too.

The choices that you have made – the right ones – have paid off. From here on in, you're going to be a permanent fixture in the pro peloton. And with the considerable pay-rise that's come with your contract extension, it's time to consider replacing that modest little flat of yours…

Well done! You've earned a two-year deal!

Your legs make the decision for you, and you drop off the back of the line, exhausted, cruising the last few kilometres to the finish.

Your team finishes third, which no one seems too thrilled about, and one of the *directeurs sportifs* pulls you aside that night and explains that they require 100 per cent effort from you, 100 per cent of the time. You counter by explaining that you thought you could be more useful later in the race, but he reminds you that it was your time-trialling ability that got you a place on the team in the first place.

You dwell on that word 'was' later that evening. You still need a new contract, and are kept awake for most of the night worrying that it might not be forthcoming.

To rub salt into the wound, a few days later you crash on a slippery, wet descent. The result: a broken collarbone – and a free flight home.

You return to your flat, feeling somewhat miffed and rejected that your one shot at superstardom consisted of just a handful of races, two major crashes and no real opportunity to prove your worth at the highest level.

A week later, you're informed that your contract will not be extended, which – if you're honest with yourself – is no great surprise on the back of what's been a pretty dismal season.

You quickly get snapped up to lead a domestic team on a very decent wage for the following season, but the damage is done, and your motivation across the off-season is at rock bottom.

But hey – at least you gave it a shot. If only there was some way that you could give it another go…

Game over

In late August, you head to the World Ports Classic – a new, two-day race in the Netherlands – which you were never originally down to ride, and which doesn't particularly suit your skills.

It's another uneventful race for your team, despite your best efforts, and, on the final night, your *directeur sportif* comes to your hotel room to tell you that he's sorry, but that the team is restructuring for the following season, and your contract will not be renewed. You thank him for everything, and part ways amicably, but you find it hard to hide your disappointment in the days that follow.

You're cheered up temporarily by a call from your country's federation selecting you for the road squad for the world championships in Florence, Italy, in September, where you finish what is a hilly road-race course well down the field.

A year in the top tier of professional bike racing is not to be sniffed at, but you can't help thinking that you deserved a better crack of the whip…

Game over

Ellis Bacon is the former deputy editor of *Procycling* magazine, and has also written for *Cycling Weekly*, *Cycle Sport* and *Cyclist*. As a freelance writer, he has written for a number of national newspapers and magazines, and often appears on television and radio to talk about professional cycling. He is the author of *World's Ultimate Cycling Races* and *Mapping Le Tour* (Collins), and translated Bjarne Riis's autobiography, *Riis: Stages of Light and Dark* (Vision Sports Publishing), from Danish to English. He is co-editor of *The Cycling Anthology*.

12

One consequence of the fall of Lance Armstrong is that every dominant performance comes under the microscope.

Having won consecutive editions of the Tour de France, with two different riders, Team Sky find themselves in the spotlight.

Jeremy Whittle has asked the relevant questions of Team Sky – but doesn't feel he has yet had all the answers.

GLASS HALF EMPTY

BY JEREMY WHITTLE

Ben Affleck is a magnificent, chiselled hunk of a man. I know this because we bumped into each other – or, rather, I bounced off him – as he strode purposefully through the lobby of the Covent Garden Hotel one night in the autumn of 2012, his entourage fussing in his wake.

Big Ben didn't flinch, but I'd swear his jaw moved just a little as he mumbled, 'Sorry, man.' Affleck was in town for the British premiere of *Argo*, the acclaimed Oscar-winning hostage drama. Personally, I prefer the thriller *Gone Baby Gone*, his first directorial outing, with a brilliant cast, led by his impossibly cute brother, Casey.

Gone Baby Gone is far more complex than *Argo*. It's a divisive and shocking movie that asks huge moral questions: is a child born into a dysfunctional family better off staying with its birth parents, even if they are totally deficient, or being removed to live with adoptive parents who can offer it a far better shot at happiness and success?

In other words, would you rather be lost in the

Boston urban badlands, or be brought up in the fragrant hill-country with kindly Morgan Freeman?

Maybe, if he'd been so inclined, Affleck would have had a take on the weighty moral questions about to be tackled in a small meeting room in the Covent Garden Hotel. As he headed towards Soho, equally big issues were about to be discussed in the hotel's basement: crime and punishment, redemption and repentance, forgiveness and tolerance.

Two hours earlier, I'd had an unexpected call from Team Sky's Fran Millar, inviting me, and several others, to a press gathering with Dave Brailsford. A handful of hacks, maybe half a dozen of us, had dropped everything to be there, anticipating big news. We were all expecting a cull of Team Sky staff, after Brailsford had instituted a series of internal interviews in the wake of new doping allegations over former team medical consultant Gert Leinders.

We had the names of those whose careers were founded in Generation EPO — those connected to Riis, Armstrong, Festina, Cofidis, TVM and the others — on our minds. You didn't have to search for long in Sky's coaching staff to find the most obvious names — Sean Yates, Steven de Jongh, Bobby Julich.

But, instead, Brailsford, flanked by the team's press and communications officers Millar and Chris Haynes, sat before us and reiterated the team's pledge of zero tolerance.

'Team Sky has zero tolerance and is 100 per cent

clean,' he says. As we sit and listen, we can't help wondering when he will talk of further dismissals from Team Sky for those whose past is about to catch up with them.

Instead, we're left pondering what happens next to sports director Yates – mentor, team-mate and confidant to Lance Armstrong and director of Team Sky during Bradley Wiggins's glory year of 2012 – and what happens to 'Class of 1998' sports directors De Jongh, once of the TVM team, or to Julich, of the Motorola, Cofidis and CSC teams.

For a team that never stopped proclaiming its adherence to zero tolerance, contracting Leinders, it had become clear, had been something of what Brailsford would call a 'reputational risk'. The problem was that much the same could have been said of Yates, Julich, and De Jongh. Yates denies any involvement in or knowledge of doping.

Of course, just because you were there, alongside others as they reached for the medicine jar, doesn't mean you did 'it'. But the time for ambiguity had long gone. People needed to know the unvarnished truth. If cycling's brave new world was to amount to anything, then that was the starting point.

Yet despite his pivotal role in saving the career of David Millar – Fran Millar's brother – Brailsford isn't interested in his staff issuing tearful confessionals and seeking hand-wringing rehabilitation. Dopers, he says, past or present, redeemed or repentant, have no place at Team Sky. All the staff will be interviewed, one by one, and ordered to reveal any skeletons in closets.

'If someone has a past, and they're lying, the likelihood of it coming out is high,' he says. 'The truth is going to come out, and it could be painful for us. If we have to start from square one, so be it.'

Only days later, after the 2013 Tour de France presentation in Paris, the media encircled Chris Froome as he stood backstage at the Palais des Congrès. Had he been interviewed by Sky as part of their re-affirmation of zero tolerance?

'It was very straightforward,' Froome said. '"Have you done anything? Are you likely to be linked to anything?" "No, no, no." "Okay – sign here." It was pretty straightforward. I wish it was that simple for everybody on the team.'

At the end of October, Yates, described as a 'valuable colleague' by Brailsford, left Team Sky for 'purely personal reasons'. There were some references to a family reconciliation and to the Englishman's failing health (although it was common knowledge that he had been suffering with cardiac problems for several years).

Both Steven de Jongh and Bobby Julich confessed to doping, and also left, while rider Michael Barry confessed and retired in one fell swoop.

As for Leinders, by now long gone, his reputation just got worse as time went on, as the steady drip-

drip of allegations and confessions trickled out of a
motley crew of former Rabobank riders.

And in light of that – the banishment of legions
of others as damaged goods, the failed due diligence
allied to the revelation that Sky's stance of zero tolerance had failed – that's when you are reasonably
entitled to also question the management's judgment
and processes.

Yates's old-school relationships, particularly with
Armstrong, but also with Bruyneel and Riis, had
always been a double-edged sword, long before
USADA blew the Texan's house down. Yes, his
lengthy CV proved Yates knew the ropes, that he
could cut it in the Grand Tours. It demonstrated
his depth of knowledge, but it also posed serious
questions about just how much he had really known
of the pro scene's dark side.

* * *

March in the south of France, and Paris-Nice is
wending its way towards the Côte d'Azur. There
are deep banks of snow lining the final two or three
kilometres of the wooded climb to the Montagne de
Lure. A freezing Mistral howls around the finish line
and clouds swirl over the mountainside.

Wearing every item of clothing we can pull on,
we slither and slide our way through the slush, and
stand shivering on the finish line. Then we wait.

Garmin-Sharp's highly rated Andrew Talansky is on the verge of his breakthrough moment. He's leading Paris-Nice with just three stages to go. The relentless Team Sky, though, have other plans.

The British team make Talansky pay for his naïvety. His foolhardy and mis-timed attack, three kilometres from the finish, is a dire mistake, and Richie Porte punishes it, rising out of the saddle, bare-armed in the icy air, before soloing clear to a stage win and the race lead.

Porte, surrounded by Sky team-mates, leads from the front on the next day's 220-kilometre stage. On Sunday afternoon, he wins the time trial stage to Col d'Éze to become the first Australian to win 'The Race to the Sun'.

It's not an unexpected victory, but Porte's time-trialling performance raises eyebrows. And so, as ever, the questions of Team Sky begin once more.

How could he explain such dominance? 'Extreme success comes from extreme hard work,' Porte says. 'We train extremely hard. Look at the recruiting over the past three years: they're all very strong riders. It's tall poppy syndrome.'

Asked to compare Sky with his old team, Saxo-Bank, whose director, Bjarne Riis, once told the Australian that he was too heavy to be an elite professional, Porte says that Sky adopt 'a totally different approach' to the more 'traditional' Riis.

Twenty-four hours earlier, Porte's friend and

team-mate, Froome, had won the summit finish to
Prati di Tivo in Tirreno-Adriatico. Sky were running
riot across the Mediterranean. And as they did so,
their riders were being asked more and more of the
same questions.

Back in March, Froome was yet to weary of the
cross-examinations. 'There's no secret,' he says. 'It's
just continuing to work the way we worked in the
last few years: training, measuring the training and
going back and doing it again. It's about getting the
basics right.'

* * *

Philippe Maire, leaning against the counter of his
bike shop in Cagnes-sur-Mer, festooned with Lance
Armstrong memorabilia, laughs derisively when we
tell him we're journalists. After initially fobbing us
off, his interest – or is it vanity? – is pricked by the
thought of talking to a British national newspaper.

'Okay – give me five minutes,' he says. 'We can
have a coffee.' He gestures to the pavement tables a
few yards away.

If you believe Tyler Hamilton, the Côte d'Azur
bike-shop owner is the semi-mythical 'Motoman' –
the drugs mule for Lance Armstrong and Hamilton,
among others, named in Hamilton's award-winning
book, *The Secret Race*.

At first, Maire, who Hamilton said delivered drugs

to the US Postal Service team's hotel by motorcycle, is a little lost for words.

'This is my little corner of my town,' he says as we sit at the bar next door to his shop. 'I love cycling and I like the quiet life. I like my job – that's it. I am not Motoman.

'I have never worked with a motorbike with any teams,' Maire says, refuting the allegations made by Hamilton. 'Never. It's a fantasy.'

But he's more open about his close friendship with Yates. Until last autumn, when Maire's relationship with Team Sky's former sports director became common knowledge, Sky riders – including Froome and Porte – were regular visitors to Maire's shop.

'Sean is very respectable,' Maire, who spent last New Year at Yates's home in Sussex, says. 'He's a strong guy, brave – like a brother to me. But then with all these sensational stories, they tried to stain Sean's reputation. They made all the stories up, transformed it all. They had no proof – it was just "blah-blah-blah". I can't stand to see Sean's reputation dirtied.

'Eighty per cent of the riders who live in Nice visit me,' he claims. 'The riders know me because I'm a good mechanic – not because of anything else. Sean brought some Sky riders here – because I was able to help them with 'O' rings – and they came here to get adjustments made.

'Froome and Porte came here,' Maire continues. 'But now that's stopped because, after all the fuss about Sean being with me, Brailsford banned any contact with me.

'But,' says Maire, his voice rising, 'it's all false. Completely untrue. Sean has never used EPO. After that, I can't say that he's never taken anything in his life, but one day he said to me, "You know, Philippe, we're seeing a generation where there's a lot of EPO." But Sean…' – and Maire spits on the pavement as he says it – '… has never used EPO. And never trafficked in it either. Sean is the most respectable person I know in cycling.'

But it's hard for Maire to conceal his reverence towards the riders and his apparent ambivalence towards doping.

'You don't have to dope, but if you don't, it's tricky. If you're not good enough, you're not good enough. If you take a little dope, you'll be better, but you'll still not be good enough,' he claims.

Every now and then, Maire, who once had ambitions of his own towards professional racing, had trained with Armstrong.

'Lance was at such a level – maybe doping improves that level – he was the strongest. I knew Lance after he'd been pro for a month. I ate at his home, we rode together – I had a good relationship with all the American riders in Nice.

'Lance was very good. He was a champion without doping. I can't say that he would have won the Tour, but Lance was good enough to beat any rider.

With Lance clean and the others clean, I think he would always have won.'

Afterwards, Maire happily poses for photographs outside the shop. When the photographer chooses an angle that shows his motorbike in the background, Maire laughs indulgently.

'Ah, yes,' he smiles. 'I know what you're up to.'

* * *

Nobody should ever doubt Dave Brailsford's capacity for hard work. He leads by example and Team Sky's principal is unrelenting, his schedule brutal. No stone is left unturned. Work comes first, and everything else – family, friendships – comes second.

But there are some things even he can't control – some things that no matter how hard he tries, he can't change. Like the perception in cycling that if you win too often, then there must be 'something' going on.

So how, post USADA investigation, can you gain credibility with the media, increase the public's confidence, when all they do is find reasons to doubt you? You bring in the witch-finder general: the man who brought down LA, the Mafia Don, the man whose reputation as a truth-seeker, an exposer of corruption in sport, is now seen as unimpeachable. You bring in David Walsh.

Brailsford says that his invitation to Walsh, to join

Team Sky on the road at the Giro d'Italia and then the Tour de France, came out of bonhomie towards the Irishman and an enthusiasm to prove to him how much the sport had changed, post Puerto, Landis, Armstrong. That may be true, but there's also little doubt that approbation from Walsh would silence those who still doubt Team Sky – even if it would never be enough to quell Paul Kimmage's bottomless well of cynicism.

Yet Walsh is a discreet presence at the 2013 Tour de France. As far as I can tell, he doesn't come to press conferences, press rooms, or finish lines. I only spot him three times. First, in Marseille, he winds down the rear window of Chris Haynes's car and mutters a strangled 'hello', then we come upon him strolling alongside Brailsford, as we drive up the road to the summit of Mont Ventoux.

As we pull over, Walsh carries on walking, but Brailsford stops to shake hands and say hello. After a couple of minutes he heads off, saying with a sly smile, 'Better catch up with my mate...'

My final sight of Walsh is of him following Froome and Brailsford to the team bus, all of them clutching champagne flutes, outside Sky's hotel in Annecy, a few hours after Froome had sealed victory.

It's fair to say that Brailsford got pretty tasty with me earlier in the year when I accused Sky of giving Walsh preferential treatment. But of course, seeking the best possible outcome for their agreement with him, they gave Walsh all the access he wanted – and a glass of champagne on the bus. For most of the time the rest of the media were restricted to press conferences and finish lines. That seems pretty preferential to me.

At the end of his time with the team, Walsh gave Sky a clean bill of health. He had asked a lot of questions and been given satisfactory answers. He had looked them in the eye and sought the truth. Sky weren't perfect, he concluded, but they deserved our trust and faith. Given what we know of Team Sky right now, I think that's probably a fair assessment.

But, unfortunately, there were other questions unasked and it is a shame to think that these may not have been put to Sky by a journalist with such privileged access. Maybe they were discussed and Walsh deemed them unworthy of publication, but, as far as I know, they remain unanswered.

There are questions over the exact circumstances of Yates's departure and his history, of confidentiality agreements with past employees, of Sky's process of due diligence on new employees, of Froome and Porte's visits to Philippe Maire, of Sky's decision not to join the MPCC (Mouvement pour un Cyclisme Crédible/Movement for Credible Cycling), of their hypothetical use of products banned by the MPCC but not by WADA, of IV or syringe usage (both supposedly monitored by the UCI) for recovery.

Those questions and others were sent directly to

Brailsford in July. He has yet to respond. The answers will not prove either guilt or innocence of any supposed wrongdoing, but they are indicative of Sky's willingness to embrace transparency.

No secrets, then – well, apart perhaps from the ill-advised visits to Philippe Maire. Not that he's Motoman, you understand – because he's not.

Ultimately, I'm sorry Brailsford, Froome and Porte have been offended by the questions – many admittedly lame and repetitive and poorly phrased – directed their way this year. But such tedious duties are the lot of those dominating a sport that remains deeply traumatised. There's no point in resenting that.

Team Sky's irritation climaxed with Brailsford, in a mid-Tour press conference in Orange, urging the media to act as a collective and to come up with some fresh ideas. That suggestion was briefly considered by some before being dismissed by the majority as Brailsford's attempt to manipulate the media narrative. The general sentiment was, 'Yes, these are sometimes boring and repetitive questions, but read the small print, guys, because when you lead the Tour de France, it's part of the job description...'

Perhaps it would help, too, if professional athletes refrained from telling us how hard they work – a plea that has unfortunate echoes of the Armstrong years. 'People ask me what I'm on...'

Nobody doubts your work ethic. Don't use those early starts and late finishes to dodge the issues. Don't hide behind 'It's all down to hard work.' These days, it sounds a little like 'I've never tested positive.'

Teachers work hard, nurses work hard, firemen work hard – why, even journalists and political representatives work hard. We expect them all to be accountable and ethical, and we expect it of you, too. So maybe it's time to get used to it.

* * *

It was hardly a surprise that Chris Froome won the 2013 Tour de France. In fact, it would have been more of a shock if he had failed. Yet, within cycling, there remains this air of lingering resentment against Sky. Where does it come from?

The connections to the Murdoch empire? The supposedly heavyweight budget and the black, overly corporate, slightly menacing image? The conspiracy theories? The constant sledging from caricatured cheese-eating surrender monkeys such as FDJ team manager Marc Madiot?

'Bah, je n'aime pas les Sky…'

In the ethical stakes, there's no doubt the Sky team's PR could be better. Their image suffers against that of Garmin, who are seen as the friendly, anti-corporate goofballs of anti-doping – something that's probably as carefully cultivated as wearing all black, all day. Compare the reactions of the world at large to successes from Garmin and victories from Team Sky and it tells you all you need to know. Ryder Hesjedal wins a brutal Giro d'Italia or Dan Martin dominates in April and wins the hardest Classic of them all – the media laps it up and hails it as evidence that cycling is cleaning up its act.

The comparisons with Garmin irritate the hell out of Brailsford, who will always insist publicly he would never structure a team around repentant ex-dopers, even if privately he may be more pragmatic.

In a way, he's in a dreadful bind. The more Sky win, the more pressure he will come under. But why should he be ashamed of trying to win every race his team starts? Surely that's the whole point.

Does anybody really doubt that Team Sky is the best Grand Tour team, with the most driven and demanding figurehead, the best forward planning and, in Froome, a rider whose cold ambition may yet take him to multiple Tour de France wins?

But maybe Sky should wear some happy colours. Maybe Dave Brailsford should grow a beard or wear a wacky hat in the evenings. Maybe he should be on Twitter, posting pictures of his fishing holidays.

Or is that the sound of him swearing and calling me names?

Jeremy Whittle covered the Tour de France for the 20th time in 2013, writing for *The Times* and *The Sunday Herald*. He is the author of *Bad Blood: the secret life of the Tour de France*, and collaborated with David Millar on his autobiography, *Racing Through the Dark*.

13

In 2013, the Tour of Britain celebrated its tenth edition.

The event also marked the return to form of Bradley Wiggins.

Lionel Birnie charts the rise of the Tour of Britain, sees an emotional homecoming for Dave Brailsford, meets Nigel Mansell and ponders the significance of the full English breakfast.

THE TOUR OF BRITAIN AT TEN

BY LIONEL BIRNIE

A fortnight after winning his first Olympic gold medal, Bradley Wiggins was back in his home town hoping to put on a show. It was early September 2004 and the first edition of the new, reborn Tour of Britain was reaching its conclusion with a circuit race around Westminster. The crowd was big by the standards of the day, but the occasion felt like a cycling event rather than a sporting event. Cycling had yet to make the quantum leap into the mainstream.

Wiggins, 24 years old, wearing the green and white colours of his French Crédit Agricole team, went clear midway through the race, joining forces with three other riders in a breakaway that lasted a few laps.

'Go on Bradley!' they shouted. 'Wiggo' had not yet been born.

A short distance from the finish line, Dave Brailsford – then, as now, British Cycling's performance director – watched in virtual anonymity. No one asked for his autograph.

With two laps to go, Wiggins tried again, opening

a small gap before being caught as the bell rang. He had wanted to win in London, but it was not to be. Italy's Enrico Degano took the sprint at the finish and the first Tour of Britain ended without a British stage winner or a home rider in the top ten overall.

Nine years later, the tenth edition of the Tour of Britain finished in the capital. My, how it's grown.

The bell to signal the final lap was rung by Wiggins's mother, Linda. Her son, Sir Bradley Wiggins, multiple Olympic and world champion, Tour de France winner, was close to the front of the bunch, wearing the gold jersey as race leader. The crowd was two or three deep in places and stretched continuously around the eight-kilometre circuit. Mark Cavendish, of course, won the sprint.

* * *

The well-told tale of British cycling's journey from rags to riches has been mirrored by the rise of the national tour. The race has had a couple of previous, unconnected incarnations. The Kellogg's Tour ran for eight years, from 1987 to 1994, and the PruTour lasted just two years, 1998 and 1999, before title sponsor Prudential, the insurance company, withdrew.

Relying on a title sponsor had always meant races in Britain had a precarious existence. When the company that was signing the cheques had had enough, the race struggled to fill the void and, when the identity of the race had been so strongly linked to one brand, as in the cases of Kellogg's and Prudential, it was often tricky to attract new backers. Sweetspot, the company run by Hugh Roberts and Mick Bennett – the latter a bronze medallist in the team pursuit at the 1972 and 1976 Olympics – changed that model.

Capitalising on the burgeoning public sector, Sweetspot secured funding from local government and regional development agencies and forged stronger relationships with communities than previous events had managed. Once that strong base had been established, commercial partners have added funding and the event grew quickly but steadily and sustainably so that it could even survive the coalition government's decision to scrap the regional development agencies and the restructuring that followed.

But there were some nervous early moments. Towards the end of the first stage of the 2004 Tour, the bunch was almost misdirected into the flow of Manchester's rush-hour traffic. There have been a few incidents that have served to prove how challenging it can be to run an international-class stage race on this crowded island, particularly in the early years when the organisers favoured busy city-centre finishes to avoid the possibility of the race being greeted by one man and his uninterested dog.

In recent years, as the sport's popularity has reached further than the cycling-club stalwarts, the

balance has tilted the other way. No longer an in-
convenience or an event that seems to be trying to
get out of the way as quickly as possible so as not
to disrupt the school run, the Tour of Britain now
owns the roads it uses – so much so, in fact, that a
small group of protestors in Surrey complained that
cyclists are taking over their county one international
race and cyclosportive at a time.

That first race was won in impressive fashion by
Mauricio Ardila – a little-known Colombian who
clinched the two hardest stages, in Sheffield and at
Celtic Manor near Newport. Tom Boonen sprinkled
a little stardust by winning in Nottingham, and the
Tour of Britain was off and running.

LLANBERIS

Dave Brailsford grew up in the shadow of Snowdon
in North Wales. Llanberis is practically home. His
father, John — a mountaineer, rock climber and keen
cyclist — knows every hump and hollow for miles
in every direction. His mother, Barbara, still lives in
nearby Deiniolen, where Brailsford grew up.

He has a train carriage on the Snowdon mountain
railway named after him now. Earlier in the summer,
before he set off for the Tour de France, he went to
Llanberis station to unveil the Sir David Brailsford
CBE carriage. 'We've won Olympic medals, world
championships and the Tour de France. There have
been honours, awards and a knighthood but, I tell

you what, to be recognised in your home town is really special,' he said.

It was an emotional day for Brailsford when the Tour of Britain arrived in Llanberis. When the route was first unveiled, Brailsford couldn't quite believe it. 'I know the roads round here like the back of my hand,' he said. 'This is where I first rode a bike, where I trained before going to France to race.'

For such a pragmatic man – someone who, publicly at least, gives the impression that he recites Kipling's poem, If, nightly so he can treat those impostors, Triumph and Disaster, both the same – the emotional and geographical significance of that stage win must have felt peculiar.

That afternoon, Mark Cavendish won his first stage of the 2013 race, and Bradley Wiggins successfully defended the race lead. These were two of the men who had taken British Cycling to the summit of cycling's Snowdon. Brailsford had managed them, cajoled them, calmed them and fired them up. Now he would be able to take an hour or so to pop round to his mum's for a cup of tea.

'Welcome home, Dave,' someone said from the behind the barriers. 'Thanks. It's good to be back.'

* * *

The Tour of Britain has always peddled a neat line in the incongruous. This year, there was the sight of

Wiggins time trialling past the elephants at Knowsley Safari Park. In Llanberis, Cavendish followed Wiggins to face a small collection of journalists in an upstairs room in the Snowdon visitor centre while downstairs hikers and mountain bikers warmed themselves with a cup of tea and a toasted sandwich in the cafeteria. It's hard to imagine two sports stars with equivalent global standing in more low-key surroundings. It was like Liam Gallagher following Damon Albarn on stage at the local community centre during the height of Britpop.

There was a particularly arresting sight in the finishing straight in Llanberis. Stepping away from the VIPs in the hospitality tent, Nigel Mansell took a seat next to the barriers, held his cup of coffee in both hands, for warmth as much as anything else, and watched the race unfold on the big screen in front of him, despite the deafening, incessant commentary from the speaker above his head.

That's Nigel Mansell, the 1992 Formula One world champion – a sporting superstar in his own right. Like Cavendish and Wiggins, Mansell has won the BBC's Sports Personality of the Year award, although it should be pointed out that his victory, like those by Nick Faldo and Steve Davis, has been cited as a case to substitute the word personality for achievement, or something similar.

Mansell is president of UK Youth – a charity that seeks to encourage young people to raise their aspirations and realise their potential. After he retired from motor racing, Mansell's first passion was golf. He bought a course in Devon – not far from Sidmouth, where stage five of the 2013 Tour of Britain started – and played on the European Seniors Tour. More recently, cycling has arrested his attention. In 2012, he rode from John O'Groats, the north-easterly tip of Scotland, to Paris to raise money and awareness for UK Youth's work.

'For someone who's had the injuries I've had over the years, and the age I am now [he's 60], to ride 1,300 miles from John O'Groats to Paris was incredibly challenging… Really, really challenging,' he says. 'But there's no doubt that we have raised the profile of UK Youth by doing events like that. We wanted to make the charity more visible and cycling came on the radar as a way to do that. Then we set up the professional cycling team – which is independent from the charity; it's owned and sponsored by the Mansell family – to promote the charity further.

'We've evolved as a race team, we've won the Tour Series in Britain, we've won the Rás in Ireland [with Marcin Bialoblocki] and the English version of Paris-Roubaix [the Rutland-Melton Classic] with Ian Wilkinson, and now we'd like to take it to the next level.'

With the on-off talk of Formula One driver Fernando Alonso taking over the Euskaltel-Euskadi team's UCI WorldTour licence finally biting the dust,

Mansell might yet reach the pinnacle of cycling before the Spaniard.

'There's no doubt we've been a victim of our own success, in a way,' he says. 'We need a title sponsor to take the team to the next level, and there's no question that if we could get a multinational that believed in the work UK Youth does to come on board, to spread the word not just of their company but also of UK Youth, it would be a fantastic partnership. You only have to look at Bradley and Mark to see how inspirational cycling can be for young people.'

* * *

The Tour of Britain has revealed more than the odd gem in its time, and a glance back at the results of the previous nine races throws up some names that stand out now even though they were less remarkable then. The 2006 race is the one that demonstrates the point most boldly. Martin Pedersen of CSC won overall, and, although his career has not reached such heights since, some others have.

Cavendish won the points competition, Andy Schleck, then a callow, stick-thin 21 year old with a much more famous older brother, took the king of the mountains jersey and Johan Vansummeren, winner of Paris-Roubaix in 2011, clinched the sprints prize. No wonder race director Mick Bennett is so fond of telling people: 'You saw them here first.'

CAERPHILLY

The An Post team car sweeps into the car park with a cartoonish flourish and the door swings open. Out of the driver's side jumps Kurt Bogaerts, the team's sports director. A man with a handheld camera gets out of the passenger door, his lens trained on Bogaerts.

Although his eyes are hidden behind dark sunglasses, the quavering lip betrays his emotions. He says a few words in Belgian-accented English, but he's fighting a losing battle with the tears.

'Like I said today, it's a family. Everybody is really happy with this because everybody worked for it. I know at home Sean, he will be really happy with this. It's the best day of the team after so many years.'

Sam Bennett, a 22-year-old Irish rider, has just won stage five at Caerphilly Castle in Wales, bumping more illustrious opponents Wiggins and Dan Martin out of the way as he careered round the final bend (he later sought out both Wiggins and Martin to apologise) and outsprinting the rest.

For the An Post-Chain Reaction Cycles team, this is a huge moment – hence Bogaerts' tears.

The team, which is owned by Sean Kelly, has made a habit of producing promising riders and sending them off to better things. Over the years they have seen Daniel Lloyd, Matt Brammeier, Gediminas Bagdonas and Andrew Fenn, among others, move on to bigger things.

But Sam Bennett's victory means that little bit more, as Bogaerts explains.

When he was a youngster Bogaerts lived in Merchtem, not far from Sean Kelly's Belgian home. Everyone knew Kelly – King Kelly – the winner of Milan-San Remo, Paris-Roubaix, Liège-Bastogne-Liège, the Vuelta a España and the green jersey at the Tour de France on four occasions. Kelly was hugely popular in Belgium, particularly in Flanders, where they recognised his toughness and adopted him as one of their own. But Kelly had a reputation for being taciturn. He wasn't unfriendly, exactly, but he wasn't the most approachable.

Bogaerts, 16 years old and with dreams in his head, plucked up the courage to knock on Kelly's door to ask if he could go training with him. 'The first two times I knocked he wasn't home. The third time, he was, so I asked him,' says Bogaerts.

Kelly said: 'Be here at nine o'clock in the morning,' before closing the door.

Bogaerts clearly didn't make a nuisance of himself on that first ride. He didn't pepper Kelly with questions and fill the air with irritating jabber. Instead, he selected his moments to prise some information out of Kelly, who responded with some advice that he himself would have dismissed out of hand. 'He told me to concentrate on my studies, get some qualifications and then think about cycling when I had something behind me.'

Although Bogaerts was a good rider, he didn't make it to the professional ranks, so he continued with his studies, began teaching engineering and then worked for a company that makes parts for aeroplanes before another opportunity came his way.

Cycling Ireland and Kelly wanted to base their team in Belgium and Kelly agreed Bogaerts would make the perfect sports director. Even now, the riders live in shared houses, training together and travelling together. Bogaerts, a youthful 36, with copper-coloured hair that seems to be an homage to his boss, runs the team on a day-to-day basis but consults with Kelly several times a week.

Kelly was thought of as the Belgian who happened to be born in Ireland, in Carrick-on-Suir to be precise. Bennett was born in Wervik, in west Flanders, but was brought up in Carrick-on-Suir. His father, Michael, was a footballer who played for Waterford United and had a spell playing in Belgium.

As a junior he rode for Carrick Wheelers (the original club, rather than the rebel offshoot Carrick Wheelers set up by Tony Ryan, which Kelly rode for). Throughout his teenage years, the locals would compare him to Kelly, which is a heavy burden for anyone.

'He's a talent but he had some difficulty stepping up from junior to under-23 level,' says Kelly of his would-be successor. 'They're always calling him the next Sean Kelly, which isn't easy for him to live up to.

He was very good as a junior but when he moved up the wins didn't come so easily. He gets very nervous before races and Kurt has been working hard with him to persuade him not to rely on his sprint. He can be more than a sprinter, he can get over the hills. But Kurt has always been on to him to be aggressive and not to wait for the sprints.'

The following morning in Sidmouth, Bogaerts is sticking little pieces of paper to the top tube of each of the bikes with a note of where each sprint and climb fall on the route. The cameraman who filmed his emotional response to the previous day's win had uploaded the clip to YouTube. 'Kurt wasn't sure about it,' he says. 'He said: "People aren't going to laugh, are they?"'

One of the team's riders, Mark McNally, a Scouser, says: 'Nah, it shows he's got a heart... We were beginning to doubt it.'

* * *

Wiggins was back on form in more ways than one. He rode like a Tour de France champion, with a confidence we have not seen since the summer of 2012. And, off the bike, the sparkle had returned to his eyes and the quick wit to his lips.

After pushing things to the limit in the time trial at Knowsley, despite the wet weather, he joked that he was prepared to take risks because if he ended up in hospital it wouldn't be far for Mrs Wiggins to visit.

After the stage at Llanberis, he paid tribute to Josh Edmondson, Sky's first-year professional who had lit up the race on Caerphilly mountain 12 months previously but had settled into a solid support role. 'He's been brilliant all year,' he said. 'You only have to look at him on the bike; he's got a lot of class. I don't want to big him up too much but he could be the next Tour de France winner in a few years.'

At Caerphilly, he remarked on the calibre of racing at the Tour of Britain these days. 'Every day is difficult and it's been the toughest edition of the race I've done. Only five years ago we would spend every night in the bar until two o'clock in the morning. Now you just wouldn't get away with it.'

That made my face go slightly hot. Five years ago, in 2008, Wiggins came to the Tour of Britain just after another triumphant Olympic Games in Beijing. I was working for a magazine at the time, and we thought it would be a good idea to ask Wiggins if he'd like to join us for a Chinese meal to celebrate his success.

I know. Written down in black and white, I can see it was a bad idea, but at the time it seemed great.

Wiggins was a good sport, happy perhaps to get out of the confines of a sterile chain hotel for the evening. But the evening was a disaster. The relationship between Wiggins and our photographer, which is crucial to make things like this work, just didn't click. The service was terrible, the food lukewarm, the atmosphere of a Chinese restaurant in Taunton on a rainy Monday night non-existent. After the photographer had left, he loosened up a bit and we had another beer, then another, and then some more until I'd lost count. After one for the road in a neighbouring pub, we poured ourselves into a taxi and dropped him off at what we hoped was the hotel we'd collected him from. I can remember thinking: 'Thank goodness I don't have to ride a stage of the Tour of Britain tomorrow.'

The following morning, my colleague and I hauled our hangovers to the first climb of the day and waited for the race. Wiggins was sitting last man in the bunch – although that wasn't actually much of a surprise; he often raced right at the back – and as he caught sight of us on the side of the road, I found myself making a guilty gesture that I hoped he interpreted as: 'We didn't force you to drink all those beers.'

HAYTOR

By Friday morning in Sidmouth, on the south Devon coast, it had stopped raining. In fairness, it had stopped by the time the race reached Caerphilly Castle, after almost five days of constant rain, but now the sun was actually out and everyone's mood was bright and buoyant.

I'm introduced to Geert Van Bondt, the sports director for the Garmin-Sharp team, who is to be my guide for the day. Van Bondt is a 42-year-old Belgian, as bald as Dave Brailsford, and with a smile always ready to flash across his face. I've been told he has something of an obsession with full English breakfasts – a subject never too far from my lips either.

We get in the car and follow the bunch out of Sidmouth.

Van Bondt retired at 34, after an 11-year career spent mostly with small Belgian teams, but with a couple of memorable years at TVM and an equally memorable spell with the American Mercury squad, though not quite for the same reason.

His best result was victory at Ghent-Wevelgem, the Belgian Classic, in 2000. Most of the rest of his career was spent working for Peter Van Petegem. The pair went to the same school and raced together at TVM and Mercury. Other than his own stand-out victory, Van Bondt remembers with most fondness Van Petegem's first victory in the Tour of Flanders in 1999. 'I brought Van Petegem up in the wind, I spent all day riding in the wind and I was still with the lead group all the way to the Muur,' he says, referring to the often decisive climb in Geraardsbergen which, in their wisdom, the Tour of Flanders organisers excised from their route a couple of years ago.

Van Bondt lives in Ninove – 'Near where the Tour of Flanders used to finish. The proper Tour of

Flanders.' Retirement felt premature to Van Bondt. 'I wanted to carry on for another two years, but I got sick and was injured, and there was no contract for me,' he says. 'So I started working as a sales manager for a brewery, selling Primus beer. I had to visit seven pubs a day. In the first one, I'd have a coffee, then another coffee at the next, then maybe a glass of water. By the fourth or fifth pub, I'd have a beer. Then someone would come ·in and ask about the cycling and we'd have a round of beers. Then he'd call his friend and say, "Hey, the winner of Ghent-Wevelgem is in the pub," and we'd have three more beers. By the time I got home, I'd had ten beers. In the end, my wife said: "You have to make a decision, because this is not healthy."

'Then I worked for the Eddy Merckx bicycle firm for a while, and that was okay until they said: "Everyone has to take turns to clean the toilets." Okay, look, I'm sorry, I was professional for 11 years, I won Ghent-Wevelgem. I don't want some young cyclist coming in and seeing me cleaning the toilets.'

He then worked for the clothing company Bioracer for a while, before being asked to work as a sports director for Quick Step at the Tour of Belgium. Later on, Van Petegem worked for Garmin as Jonathan Vaughters' adviser for the cobbled Classics, which in turn opened the door for Van Bondt. He did the Eneco Tour for Garmin, the feed-back for the riders was good and now he does around

150 days a year in the team car. The Belgian Classics are his speciality and the rest of the year he does an eclectic mix of international stage races – the Tour Down Under, the Tour of California, the Tour of Britain and the Tour of Beijing among them.

Van Bondt is glad to be back in cycling. As a rider, he did okay, but was denied his one big payday when the American Mercury team collapsed mid-season in 2001. 'I had a two-year contract – it was the biggest of my career – but I only got paid for six months. The UCI's bank guarantee gave me another three months, but in the end I only got nine months out of 24. I got a lawyer involved, and he was looking at the case, but after a while he said he needed money for expenses and I thought, "You know what? I should let this go." I saw the guy who owned the team [John Wordin] at the Tour of California and he came up and said hello as if nothing ever happened. I said to him: "Hey, can I have my money?" I think he thought I was joking.'

Having rolled out of Sidmouth and into the Devon countryside, he outlines the plan for the day. It's pretty simple. With Ireland's Daniel Martin a contender for victory at the top of Haytor, the idea is to sit tight and rely on Sky and Omega Pharma-Quick Step keeping the breakaway under control. 'As long as the gap is a minute and a half and no more at the bottom of the climb, it will work out well,' he says.

Garmin-Sharp are down to four men, having lost

Nathan Haas and Robbie Hunter in separate crashes on the second day. They are soon to lose Steele Von Hoff, their Australian sprinter, who is suffering with a bad stomach. He's dropped on the first hill, then again on the second. 'Come on Steele. You have to get back. Think of the sprint in London,' says Van Bondt, although he knows Von Hoff is most likely done for.

Later we see Jacob Rathe, who has dropped back to fetch a bottle for Martin.

'How are the legs?' Van Bondt asks.

'Yeah, good actually.'

'You see, I told you. The less you eat, the stronger you get.'

That brings us to Van Bondt's obsession with full English breakfasts. They are not something the Belgians go in for, but every time he's in Britain, Van Bondt indulges. By the end of the race, he'd managed nine full English breakfasts in ten days – skipping one only on Saturday when, he admits, he could not face another plate of sausage, bacon and egg.

What's the appeal?

'I like the combination of different ingredients,' he says, although he draws the line at eating black pudding. 'I need to know where the sausage comes from and I don't know where the big hotels get their pig's blood from…'

Back to the race and the warm weather has woken the bunch up. The pace is fierce all day. The crowds are huge. 'Like Belgium, eh?' says Van Bondt.

I spot two wonderfully British signs held up by fans. One reads: 'You're all doing really well.' The other says: 'Keep going! It's not far!'

Van Bondt takes a roundabout on the wrong side of the road and hits a speed bump a little too fast. He catches the concerned look on my face. 'Nigel Mansell would be impressed with that, no? Make sure you put that I'm a really good driver.

'It's so strange here,' he continues. 'There are no bicycle lanes. It's like no one is thinking about bicycles and yet there are all these people out.'

The Sky car just in front pulls over to the side of the road and the doors swing open. A few papers fly out and scatter in the road. 'Ah... That's the contract of Ian Stannard,' he says, dryly.

Although the stage pans out exactly as Van Bondt predicted, Martin's accelerations on the climb to Haytor come to nothing. Having ignited the race with Nairo Quintana on just about every climb, he mis-times his efforts slightly, not realising that there is a flatter section before the final steep kick to the line. Instead, Simon Yates, the Great Britain under-23 rider, calculates the finish perfectly.

There's an irony here. Yates, and his brother Adam, are being well served by Great Britain, as many of their predecessors in the Academy programme, including Mark Cavendish, Geraint Thomas and Ian Stannard were. All those riders have something in common: a proficiency and passion for track racing.

But Daniel Martin was the one that got away. There was no doubting his talent. He won the British national junior road race title in 2004, and raced for Great Britain at the world championships later that year. He forgot his shoes and had to ride the first lap in trainers while a *soigneur* went back to the hotel to get them. But at that time, before the base in Quarrata, Tuscany, was established, track racing was one of the cornerstones of the programme, and Martin was not a track rider; he was a climber.

Martin's father, Neil, was a British professional in the 1980s, and his mother, Maria, is Stephen Roche's sister. In 2006, having lined up a place at Vélo Club La Pomme in Marseille, he decided to ride for Ireland. In 2008, he was fourth overall in the Tour of Britain and since then he has gone on to win the Tour of Poland, the Tour of Catalonia, Liège-Bastogne-Liège and stages of both the Tour de France and the Vuelta a España.

* * *

Talking of full English breakfasts, as I was earlier, and having not learned a thing from our disastrous, left-field attempt to produce a magazine article the year before, at the end of the 2009 Tour of Britain we decided to take Chris Froome on a tour of the capital as part of a tongue-in-cheek initiation ceremony.

Froome, who rode the Tour of Britain for Barloworld that year, had changed nationalities from Kenyan to British some months before. He had agreed to join the new Sky team at the start of 2010 and so we thought it would be a good idea to introduce him to some of the finest things British culture has to offer. It was also around the time the Government's citizenship test was in the news, so that might have had something to do with it.

We met Froome at his hotel and took him for a ride on the London Eye. He was unfailingly polite and good-humoured despite our increasingly bewildering requests. He even offered to pay for his ticket to ride the London Eye.

We presented him with a full English breakfast. He was happy to pose for a photograph with it but wasn't too keen to actually eat anything. 'Do British people have this every morning?' he asked, looking horrified. Not every morning, Chris; we leave that to the Belgians.

We took him to a proper boozer and asked him to have a go at pulling a pint of British ale. He did pretty well too – the head was foamy but not too deep. Froome was as bemused as the barman was when he overheard me saying: 'This guy might win the Tour de France one day and wouldn't it be great to say he'd pulled a pint in your pub?'

We finished off by asking him to pose for a photograph outside the gates of Buckingham Palace wearing a novelty plastic policeman's helmet. Yes, we really did do this. We apologised to Froome at the time and I'm more than happy to do so again.

* * *

Bradley Wiggins has had a somewhat dysfunctional relationship with his home tour at times. Sometimes he's seemed bemused at the level of attention his presence attracts. In 2010, as Team Sky's first disjointed season drew to a close, and a bloodied but just-about-unbowed Dave Brailsford prepared to return to Manchester to unpick exactly what had gone wrong at the Tour, the team imploded during the Tour of Britain. Yet Wiggins and Brailsford were cheered and clapped on their backs wherever they went. This adulation mystified Brailsford, who felt at the time like that first Tour de France had been the most humiliating failure of his career.

Wiggins got into a break on the second stage, to Stoke, but, instead of attacking as planned, went back to the team car to suggest the team put their weight behind Geraint Thomas or Greg Henderson instead. In doing so, Sky missed the move, Wiggins did the bulk of the work to bring it back together again and Henderson saved the day by winning the sprint. But that, and some other bizarre decisions later in the week, led High Road's sports director Brian Holm to joke: 'Team Sky – tactics by Benny Hill.'

After his two greatest Tour de France performances, Wiggins has bowed out of his lap of honour early. After his fourth place in 2009 and his victory in 2012, he made it only as far as Stoke-on-Trent. A cynic would point out that this was also the closest the race got to his house on both occasions.

But in 2013, the focus appeared to return. Brailsford very deliberately set out the team's plan before the race, making it clear that Wiggins was the leader and that he'd be expected to perform and, if possible, win the race. The inclusion of a ten-mile time trial tilted the balance in his favour, but, with Wiggins, nothing is a given unless his mind is made up.

As the sun dipped behind the government buildings in Whitehall, making the finishing straight feel particularly cool, Wiggins arrived at the press conference for his latest gentle joust. Sky's PR man said: 'Okay guys, four-to-five minutes…'

Wiggins looked appalled. 'Forty-five minutes?'

After that, there was a pragmatism that always seems more studied than it does natural. 'The feeling at the moment is more just relief than anything else, to be honest. It's a funny one: you want to win it and when you've crossed the line you feel relief more for your team-mates that you've fulfilled the job. It is pressure for the whole week and I said I wanted to win it, put my hand up to win it.

'I train all the time, I enjoy training, I enjoy being fit, but there was an element of going through the motions in all the races early in the season. I came out this week with the commitment that I showed last year. I crashed on day two, was straight up and straight back in the bunch, unfazed by it.

'The reception the race has had, the team has had and that I've had throughout the race has been over-whelming at times, and nice to see.'

With that, he was gone – whisked away to spend the evening with his family before flying to the world championships in a private jet.

And, as he made his way along Whitehall, they chanted, like the crowd at a football match.

'Wig-go! Wig-go! Wig-go!'

Lionel Birnie is a journalist, author, publisher and cyclist. His company, Peloton Publishing, released Sean Kelly's long-awaited autobiography *Hunger* in 2013. He also collaborated with Rob Hayles on his book *Easy Rider*. Along with Ellis Bacon, he edits *The Cycling Anthology* and he fills in the rest of his time writing for newspapers and magazines. He is also a regular on the popular Humans Invent cycling podcast.